Ann Salmon has had dogs in her life ever since she enticed Mrs Drake's dachshund under the fence when she was three. After a number of years of mixed breeds, she fell for Border Collies and has owned, trained, worked and competed (occasionally winning) with them as well as breeding her own litters. Her dogs do Agility, Competitive Obedience, Flyball, Heelwork to Music, and various tricks classes, which didn't leave much time for anything else, but she managed to squeeze in yoga, bobbin lacemaking and gardening when possible, and friends and family when not in Lockdown.

This is Ann's second book, the first was a millennium project – an illustrated social history of West Chiltington during the last century.

This book is dedicated to all those who have supported Dizzy and me through all our difficulties and cheered us on when we got it right.

Neighbours who were invited in "for a coffee and to be barked at", family and friends who didn't complain when she nipped or bit them, our wonderful vet Andy, and Mark-with-the-sprats our behaviourist as well as a team of others too numerous to mention. Thank you all, from us both.

Ann Salmon

DIZZY'S DIARY

AUSTIN MACAULEY PUBLISHERS™

LONDON • CAMBRIDGE • NEW YORK • SHARJAH

A CIP catalogue record for this title is available from the British Library.

ISBN 9781398439962 (Paperback)
ISBN 9781398439979 (ePub e-book)

www.austinmacauley.com

First Published 2022
Austin Macauley Publishers Ltd®
1 Canada Square
Canary Wharf
London
E14 5AA

Introduction
Early February 2019

It was always a given that I would end up by changing the name of any dog we took in, and Lily, as she was, was no exception. Particularly as she was sick in the car on the way home from the rescue centre on Thursday afternoon, then bit my friend who was holding her in the car and, finally, peed twice on the hall carpet. This was all within the first hour or so, so Disaster she became; Dizzy for short and to save from hurting her feelings.

My wonderful Mayhem, a tri-coloured working sheepdog and the only bitch in her litter of six brothers, had died about six months before. Having had sheepdogs all my life, I was keen to get another, but not, this time, to breed my own. So, I started looking at Border Collie rescue sites, and even though I only wanted a bitch under two years old, not a big ask I thought, I couldn't find one, so I widened the search to general rescue homes.

This rescue home was canny, knowing I wanted a collie! They only showed a photo of her head to begin with; her collie head is attached to a Springer Spaniel body, with very short Corgi-type legs, a loo brush for a tail combined with a bad attitude and a tendency to bite. But when I saw her for the first time, I got eye contact and thought that there was something there to work with, even though she was such a funny-looking thing. She's a bully though, but most of that is defensive aggression because she's also very needy, and Candy (our other collie) isn't at all sure that she will tolerate her. Thankfully, we have the puppy cage which she goes in at night and when we're out, and I can put her there to cool off, as, for example, when she attacked the vacuum cleaner. Having said all that, I gave both dogs bones this morning and took them away again after a while (they can't have them too long in case they get upset tummies) and whilst she didn't like me taking the bone, and growled, she gave it up without a fight or a bite.

Candy isn't impressed, and neither is my long-suffering husband Tony, as he is still concerned that Candy will suffer as the emotionally weaker one in the relationship, but it's early days yet, so we will have to see what happens in the weeks to come.

It's nice to have two dogs again, even if one of them isn't a collie and is a bit of a problem!

The above is a copy of what I sent to the family who have been watching the 'will she/won't 'she get-another-dog' debate for a few months now, just to let them know who we got and why.

Chapter One
The First Weeks

Thursday, 7 February 2019.

When I got up this morning, I had no idea what was in store for me today; what a lot of excitement, and fright. Two people came to the kennels, my home for the last few months, and sat in the office with Laura-the-owner for ages, filling in forms and talking. Then I was picked up by one of them and we sat in the passenger seat, while the other one, who I had met before a couple of times, got into the driver's side. It's only a very small car with two seats so it was all a bit of a squash, and I was also covered with and in a lot of towels ~~ what were they expecting?

I thought it right to let everyone know what I thought of the car, and the driving, so I was sick, into my muzzle which Laura had made me wear. It was revolting. But the one who had hold of me and is called Heather thought that as I had been sick so close to home, it would be a good idea for me to walk up The Lanes to the house to walk off the nausea, and so she could clean her trousers. Everyone arrived at the front door more or less together, so Heather went on to her home and we went indoors and I needed to scent mark MY territory and let everyone know I'd arrived. So, I peed on the carpet twice, just to make sure. In the conservatory, which is just off the kitchen, they have a lovely big puppy cage (big enough for an elephant puppy, I think) which my crochet blanket from the kennels was in, so I went in there and lay down while they had tea. If it had been lighter, I could have seen into the garden as my cage was in front of the big double doors, but I could see into the kitchen and the breakfast bit as well; there's Him and Her and Candy the sable collie who is old, and I had met a few days before in a big field with Her and Laura from the kennels. We had biscuits at bedtime, and my pig's ear to chew, and then I got shut in the cage for the night after a cuddle. I barked a bit but no one took much notice, so I stopped and we all slept all night.

Friday morning was a bit scary as it was all so new; we went into the garden first thing for a pee, but Candy barked and barked and I didn't like the noise at all, so I refused to come out of my cage. She tried to coax me out, but when She put her hand in, I grumbled, quietly but firmly. She just stared at me ~ I decided to stop grumbling and when Candy had been shut in the hall and gone quiet, I went out into the garden. It's a big garden with lots and lots of smells in it. After a pee, we get a sausage roll and wait while They have breakfast; we had pilchards and veggies for our breakfast and then we went for a walk in the woods. We went on leads even though it's ever so close; the entrance to the woods is in the next lane and there are no pavements but very narrow roads, with almost no traffic, so we were there in a few minutes. Not many people or dogs about, and I was kept on my lead, which I hated so I pulled and pulled, and after about an hour, I managed to slip my collar off and ran into the car park, but came back to have a makeshift collar put on to go back home as it seemed a big wood and I didn't want to get lost.

We had a biscuit each when we got home, and They had coffee, then a fairly quiet afternoon except that I got ROARED at when I tried to go into their bedroom, so I think I'll just stay outside and bark instead. And regular visits to the garden to "be clean, girl"; not sure what it meant but I peed anyway. Then I had to go back and get shut into my cage because They went out for drinks with friends, and suddenly, it was bedtime, but no barking tonight as I was too tired.

Saturday, 9th. Same routine as yesterday but the woods are too much fun to be on a lead in, so although She had spent time making my collar tighter, I still managed to slip it and chase squirrels for ages. It is a big wood owned by The National Trust, as a lot of land round here is, with open glades, wooded hills full of squirrels, wonderful boggy bits and an open grassy common in the middle. It is bounded by two main roads, but we don't go near them. There are two areas on the walk that go near the A24, and I'm not telling anyone why, but at each one I pulled very hard to get to the road, but didn't succeed.

At the beginning of the walk, we met someone called Tony and his Springer Bertie, and another woman with her dog Ken who was a bit of a nuisance and wouldn't leave me alone. Then when I was let off the lead, I met lots and lots of dogs, but no one bothered me and I didn't bother them so although it could have been scary, She wasn't bothered so I wasn't either. I think She was a bit anxious though, as She had noticed my tail up like a scorpion's, which means *trouble*! We came home just inside the hour, for coffee and a rest, and then recall-training in the garden; I did come, but in my own good time as there was such a lot to scent and find out, which was much more interesting than She was. The we had a big beef

11

bone each in the garden, which I reluctantly had to give up when She told me to. Heather came to collect her paper and I tried to nip her. Everyone was so cross, I think I might not do it again, though I will bark and bark and fight the Henry vacuum cleaner; I don't like its noise. There was rugby on the television so a very boring evening, though I thought there might be trick training later. There wasn't.

Because it was Sunday today, I went for a walk with Him, and he had me on the Flexi lead which was a lot more fun in the woods. We didn't meet anyone except Mr and Mrs Lancing and their Corgi but no one discussed whether I was Corgi or not; I think he forgot to. I still wanted to run to the A24, and I'm still not telling why! After lunch, we went into the garden with our bones, again, and again I gave mine up without too much fuss, but I got bored as She was gardening, so got my own back by Digging A Big Hole in the little flower bed underneath the central tree in the garden. She was not pleased, so I went and dug another one somewhere else, and she wasn't please by that either, so then I Went Down to Australia with a huge hole and bulbs, corms and plants scattered everywhere. I've not seen her really cross before, and I got sent indoors even though it was such nice weather that we were all in the garden. I didn't like that at all, but after tea, I was good and got lots of praise and cuddles because I didn't go into Their bedroom, just stood in the doorway and didn't even bark. The we did some training; Sit, Down, and Back, which I didn't understand. However, I did bark from 10 pm to 11.15 because I didn't want to go in the cage at bedtime and I just needed everyone to know; we had had biscuits and Dentastix and cuddles, but I wasn't happy. No one took any notice for ages but then She came back into the conservatory and let me out and I settled down on one of the dog rugs, but I was made to go back into the cage in the end when She put the rug into it to make it comfier. I did growl and try to bite her though as She had her hand in *my* cage—not a good idea! But it's my cage and my safe space, and I'm not sharing it with anyone, not even Her.

The next morning, She and Candy played tuggie after our first-thing pees, but I do not like it when they both make growly noises, so I tried to bite them both, but She donked me on the head so I thought I'd better stop. We met loads and loads of dogs in the woods, all lovely and their owners all thought I was lovely too! Good walk, lots of treats and cuddles and squirrel smells. The plumber came but I was shut in my cage in the conservatory so couldn't get into any trouble but I made it clear that I didn't like other people in My House. After he'd gone, I scent marked the carpet where the plumber had been, and barked and grizzled for hours. Well, She said it was hours; I bet it wasn't.

Tuesday, 12th. We got a bit of cheese and half an egg each in our breakfast this morning; I think it was because She had forgotten to defrost the tripe so we had that instead! We went out with Him again as She was away all day. Tried to have another fight with Candy about the tuggie, but was shouted at and went to sulk in the hall until She came to get me. Better now. Then there was The Battle of the Sofa. I wanted to be on it and She didn't want me to be; I jumped up twice and each time got shouted at but the second time I wouldn't get off and tried to bite Her, then suddenly I was on the floor ~~ I just didn't see it coming. So, I went into my cage and sulked, but not before I'd sneaked into their bedroom and emptied all the tissues out of the waste paper basket. They didn't find out until after I was in bed, so I was safe.

We went out with Him again the next day as She was out again, and had a good walk but with fewer sniffs and more pulling. After lunch, Miles-the-garden-guru came to do some pruning and planning which meant They walked round the garden together, and She thought I might relax a bit if I went to meet him, on the lead, but I tried to bite him hard instead. Fortunately, he had on thick padded trousers so there was no real damage done so we made friends and had cuddles and a treat. She relaxed, so I tried to bite him again, but this time She was wiser and had the lead very short. After the third time I tried to have a nip at him, She took me indoors and shut me in my cage. It was the first time anyone had come into My Garden without asking me, and I didn't like it; I can cope with people in the woods, but not in my garden. And I barked all afternoon as I was cross. And scared. Then, to top a bad day, Candy and I arrived at the sitting room door together and had a scrap as to who was going through first. I won!

The next day, while She was still a bit frazzled, we went to visit Andy-the-vet; They did a lot of talking and I know it was about me as they kept looking at me even if they pretended not to. She had taken me in on a lead, but had the muzzle in her hand in case it was necessary, and Andy said that was all right and he'd tell Her if he wanted it putting on, which he didn't. She had asked him to check my spine, hips and tail as I had got very cross and upset when She tried to brush that part of me the other day; She was afraid that there might be some residual damage there from my previous experiences, but Andy said everything was all right and just continue slowly. He gave Her some pills for me, to try and reduce my tension and anxiety, and he also said I was lovely, and gave me treats; I had to sit on the scales in the vet's reception area and She said I will end up fat as butter if I get treats at this rate, but I don't care one bit!

It was even better the next day as Oliver (grandson) came round with his little daughter Chloe to see me, and I got lots more treats. Chloe is only two and sat on the floor ~ we were all in the conservatory ~ playing with toy cars which she rolled across the tiled floor to bang into the side of my cage; she thought it was great fun, but I got scared and started to grumble. Oliver just moved so he was sitting on the floor between his daughter and me, so I shut up and relaxed as Oliver is so calm, and Chloe started to play with something else. A few days later, we had even more visitors; Tony who we had met in the woods a few days earlier with his springer, and his wife Carole who came for the evening, and I was shut in my cage but the barking is getting less, I think. At least it was until the plumber arrived the next day, and again I made a real, real fuss, so got lots more treats to shut me up. This is a good game and I will continue to make a fuss so I get rewarded ~~ is that the idea? There is also someone called Llyn who comes every Thursday afternoon to do exercises with Him in the sitting room, and I am kept in my cage with the door to the cage, and to the kitchen, and to the hallway closed. I think that's a bit of overkill.

When I had been here exactly a fortnight, something dreadful happened and I don't quite know how ~ as it was a Thursday, it was His turn to take us out in the morning, and we met Heather and her dog Bouncy Bess and had a lovely walk in the woods together. Bess kept running off, but He kept me on the lead in case I did too, and at the end of a good morning we all left the woods together to come home. That was two humans and three dogs, which in these tiny footpath lanes is a bit of a squash, but we manage; at least we did until a woman and her dog came towards us. She was very stressed, exuding tension and anxiety, so just as she squeezed past us, I bit her on the leg. He was most concerned and solicitous but she shrugged him off and went home to her house in the next road. And reported me to the police.

Today, I ran away; They were frantic but I managed to find my way home which was good, They said, as it showed that I call this place Home and come back here when necessary.

Dizzy's Correspondence ~ Aka Fan Mail

10 February

Hi Ann

Oh dear, it sounds like Dizzy will be a bit of a challenge but I guess you were prepared for that. I think she has met her match in you though! We all loved reading her diary, it would be lovely to get 'the sequel' whenever you have time. Lorraine, our dog behaviourist, is always happy to talk to you if you need any advice. Good luck!

Barbara x

****

16 February

Don't worry Dizzy

She really is trying very hard to IMPROVE your life. You will have to give up eventually because SHE won't. She's not just a hard nut to crack I think she's uncrackable. Keep her on her toes, she thrives on this sort of thing but all her border collies and tiresome neighbours were defeated in the end. However, much I applaud your determination to get the better of her... perhaps it would be easier if you give in NOW... accept that you've found a lovely home 🏠 and admit defeat. It'll be so much easier in the end.

A well-wisher who knows

****

14th February

Original Message-----Have you found her? I did post a message on Facebook / Heath Common but nobody has replied. Kevin.

Reply: You are so kind; thank you very much. She finally turned up on the doorstep, which is a bonus I suppose in that she thinks of us as "home", but I have decided, dog training apart, that

I need a more modern phone! Thanks for all you did, and see you tomorrow perhaps, with her on the lead for the next fortnight!

Ann ~ 25th February

21st February

Never mind Dizzy, you'll get there I think you are doing well … just give yourself time, forget about acting Romanian and try to comprehend the English country code. The English are a funny lot altogether and we don't attack the people we meet (though often sorely tempted so to do) … It's called good manners.

My lab pal Reuben met an uncouth dog in the forest this morning, very big and no manners at all … called a malamute (? Spelling)… like a husky. Reu wisely lay down and waved his legs in the air. He doesn't do attack. He just wants to mind his own business. The malamute's owner said proudly "he's an alpha male". Stupid woman. Our opinion of her wouldn't be printable. Later in the walk it attacked a small black dog who was minding its own affairs; thankfully it wasn't injured.

It was nice to meet your new mum on Tuesday and hear about your progress. Poor Candy must have wondered just what was going on when you breezed into her peaceful domain and the man of the house also but he's used to coping with whatever comes his way. He's had years of experience.

Hope the next week goes well. Your friend Y

Candy and me in the hall during the first few days.
9 February 2019

Chapter Two
Mad March Days

Sullington Warren with the green in the centre and two
dog walkers

Friday, 1 March. What a busy day! First a friend of Hers
called Jane called in on her way to somewhere, to meet me,
and she gave me a Schmacko and lots of fuss; I was put in my
cage with the door shut whilst she got inside the house and
settled down, and I barked like anything, but went quiet as
soon as I was let out. Jane's lovely and made such a fuss of
me. She met Jane a few years ago in Sullington Warren when
she asked Her if she knew any good dog walks as they'd only

just moved house recently and didn't know the area. Thereafter, they met every Saturday in the Warren and Candy and Mayhem and She walked with Jane, and Sally and Katy who were also rescues, from Greece somewhere. They were lovely dogs and everyone had a happy time, but after She had known them a few years, Jane and her husband moved to the coast so they didn't meet as often. Then Sally died, very early, and Katy was so lost and lonely that Jane got another rescue called Rouli who is very small, even smaller than me, but a lot of fun and we all run round together. Sullington Warren is a National Trust area of mostly heathland, a big grass bowl in the middle and woodland all around the edge. Although it isn't huge, it seems big as there are so many different trees and paths and separate areas including a very boggy bit where Candy loves to get filthy, so we don't go there very often when it's been really wet.

Candy said that Mayhem had stepped on an adder there one year as the soil is so sandy and the snakes come out to bask in the early morning when we all go for walks, so on sunny days She stamps round so they can hear us coming and go and hide away somewhere. There are the remains of an old windmill on one of the hills, and beautiful yellow gorse everywhere.

Then in the afternoon, Heather called in, I think she's still a bit scared of me as, instead of putting her hand out flat to me, she kept her fingers curled into a fist, which I didn't like, so I jumped up at her which she didn't like at all. It all got a bit tense but it sorted out in the end. Everyone that comes seems to come into the conservatory for coffee and lots of chat, so I see most of what's going on. Later in the afternoon, there was lots of Recall training, with liver cake as a reward, and Sit, Down and something I still don't understand called Back. Dug up the "lawn" again, but I didn't know it was supposed to be special as it was all sandy and bumpy with very little grass, and while She was gardening I dug up another flower bed full of bulbs and plants, and when She told me to stop, I went and dug in the shrub border instead. The problem is, I need lots of attention, and so does the garden. But I get bored and the garden just grows. Liver cake at bed time; the whole house smells of liver and garlic, which I really like; She makes it especially, and if my legs were longer, I'd have it off the counter top, but until I work something out it's out of reach.

The next day, we had a wonderful walk all round Sandgate Park which included crossing the brook on a log; well, She couldn't balance to do that with me on the lead so She let me off in the belief that the fence at the end was entire, and it wasn't so I ran round the gate and was out on my own! But after a while, and I never went the 'wrong' way, She called and I came back and was put back on the lead which was a shame as there was a pond of ducks to chase if I'd been free. I did lots of Recalls on the lead, too. Sandgate Park used to be owned by Horsham District Council, but they gave responsibility for it to The Sandgate Conservation Trust who maintain it, cutting back the Rhododendron ponticum (the tiresome purple one) and encouraging the heathers and other trees. There is a pond/lake by the gate, and lots of little streams; when it rains, which it has hardly done since I got here, the ground turns to black leaf squelch and we all get very dirty even though we stay on the sandy dirt paths. It's mostly wood and heath land with almost no open grass, but there are lots, and lots, and lots of squirrels. It is a short walk from home so we still don't need to arrive by car, we can just go down the twitten and along some of the residential roads, which aren't designated roads really, just bridleways so there is little traffic. When we got home, late, we had the bones again, and They had lunch. After a quiet afternoon chopping wood and gardening, David and Anneli (son and daughter-in-law) came round. I ignored Anneli, but I bit David three times; he scares me very much. They are all very perplexed as David loves animals and when I went and said 'Sorry', I meant it, but I am scared of him and no one can work out why, and I can't tell them. And David is Oliver's father, and I liked Oliver.

Editor's Note: Before David and Anneli left, Dizzy followed him into the kitchen in crouching pose, ready to pounce. When she bit him for the third time, he was actually walking down the hall away from her, and it was a bad bite, drawing blood. I held her collar and moved her out of the way and into the conservatory whilst David and Anneli went out of the front door. Being so much collie, she has the collie habit of biting the backs of legs, which is unfortunate! She went into her cage (refuge), and stayed there all evening and was very upset. Last thing at night, Tony took both dogs into the garden for their last-time wee, a quick affair as it was pouring with rain, came back in and gave them biscuits and Dentastix as usual and she seemed relaxed. He went off to bed but I stayed up to sort out a problem with my lace and she came into the sitting room but was very restless and wouldn't settle. Eventually (11 pm) I finished, and we all went back into the conservatory where I usually tuck her into her tartan rug, but tonight she tried to bite me too. I was in her cage, in her space, but I always am last thing, it's part of the trust-and-training

24

thing and there haven't been problems before. Questions: Is she in pain? She seemed very hyper-tense ~ is this a result of too much protein in her diet? Why was she so scared of David (6' 3", early 50s, tall but very laid back) and ignored Anneli altogether? I think I will try and make tomorrow very calm and serene with no visitors and no excitement. Every other time she has tried to go for someone there has been a reason, usually a reason I should have foreseen, but I find this inexplicable, and very worrying.

My Tartan Rug, At Bedtime
22 February

Sunday, 3rd. She is still tense and had a snap at me and Candy who got in her way. She pulled hard on her lead when Tony took her out, a situation that wasn't helped by an entire dog called Bernie trying to mount her and Candy; he should have been 'done' years ago but her owner won't hear of it, and he's only a mongrel. She was fidgety all day, barking at a woman on the television and trying to bite me when I tried to untangle a bit of her tail. This was fear not pain. She was also 'otherwise' when I put her to bed.

Monday, 4 March 2019. I think I might be a bit better today, though I barked long and hard at Cyril's bin, he had put it out for the bin men but had put it in a new place and I didn't like that. I like things to stay the same and then I don't get scared. However, when it didn't bark back, or run away, I finally gave up and came in for a biscuit. I let Her stroke me, and my tail, though I didn't like it much.

Editor's Note: For Tuesday, I will take over. After a good long walk, to allow Simon-the-handyman to get into the house and start his work and investigations, we arrived home. On the walk, we had encountered a jogger who, after Dizzy's initial lunging towards and barking at, settled down into a happy, stroking relationship. Adrenalin back down, we continued and met Rebecca out with Labrador Alfie; she was throwing sticks for him to retrieve from the lake in Sandgate Park. Dizzy's tension levels rose again and she barked and lunged, though whether from excitement or fear I wasn't sure. When we got home, I could see Simon's car was still in the drive so after taking off her muzzle and Flexi-lead, I put her in her cage with the door closed, and Simon, Tony and I had a coffee in the conservatory where the cage is. The initial barking was deafening, but eventually calmed down as no one was taking much notice of her or it. In a while, I opened the cage door and she wandered out to make a fuss of Simon and we continued to chat. After about half an hour or so, it was time for Simon to go, so he slowly wandered off towards the loo, all very calm and non-panicky. As he came out of the loo, she, who had been lying on the front door mat, went for him.

Thank goodness for the density of denim; there wasn't any real damage, but it's this unpredictability that is so unnerving. I cannot, and will not, keep her in a muzzle indoors as well as when we are out in public places, but I suppose she will have to stay in her cage while we have people in. Someone on the dog walk had suggested that she had gone for David because of his bare legs ~ we've always teased him that although he's a company director, he should have been a postman as he's always in shorts, and perhaps it was that she had been kicked by a postman in the past? Simon had on long trousers so I can only assume that she is terrified of all men, however dressed and however calm. She seems to trust us, but so far, only us. It hasn't stopped Simon making a date to come and do running repairs to the house and decorate a couple of rooms, but she will have to stay in her cage all the time he is here.

Jane came for coffee again, so lots of treats and cuddles; she is lovely. I think she must belong to the family as she comes in and out a lot; I just don't understand why this pack lets all sorts of people in to their house. Back home, I would have chased them away. But they seem to like people here, and I can't get used to that. The next day, we went for a long walk and I was off the lead, and came back, the first time. Then I thought it was rather fun to be off, but She just walked away and left me behind, so, although I didn't get within catching range, I could still see her and Candy. She caught me in the end though. I was far too woozy to concentrate on training so we skipped it and watched rugby all afternoon and slept as those pills make me dozy ~~ Dozy Dizzy!!!

Sunday turned out to be a funny day; after a walk so early it was barely light, Candy and I were put in the car and taken to Old Clayton Kennels for the day as They were going to London. I was so good and now have a fan club; they took my muzzle off and I didn't have it on at all, all day, and was lovely to everyone. They didn't even bother to give me an extra pill as I was so relaxed, but that was because I was in their house, and not having to have them in mine. More rugby when They got home and had collected us. Boring.

After a phone call to Andy-the-vet, I started my new pills last night and am cool, calm and collected today without being totally knocked off. I didn't even bother to bark much when someone drove into the driveway. However, I refused to take the capsule tonight though; they're horrible and we had such a fight about it, so I retreated into the back of my cage and wouldn't come out until I was eventually tempted by cornflakes! I love them; they're so crunchy. She won in the end, and then "forgot" to shut me in my cage, so I spent the night with Candy. The fights over the capsules continued for days as I really don't like them, but She got round it by emptying the contents into a piece of Mozzarella and squishing it all up in gravy, so I wouldn't notice. I would have been forgiven anything today though as I spent the night with Candy and we waited by the bedroom door for Them to get up, get dressed and come out. They think I'm wonderful! I've also discovered I've got a name; I'm called Dizzy which is a bit like one of the names I had before, but then She changes it sometimes to Dizzy-Wizz, or Disaster Dog, or You Daft Thing, but I know She always means me. It's nice to have a name. Back home, I used to be called *"Dispari!"* which I don't think is very nice.

Today, We Did Traffic; went for a long, long walk but with lots of lanes and minor roads and cars. The cars were so good and slowed down so I didn't bark and get scared, but DHL and other vans drove far too fast so I went barking mad; then there were lots of fields but no trees so I couldn't even bark at the squirrels. We were out for ages and had bones when we got home; it must be Friday when He gets them from the butcher. Chris-the-plumber came but I was shut outside with my bone so didn't mind, and he was shut indoors but when I had finished the bone and come indoors, it was a different matter; I got very territorial and barked for the whole few hours that he was here, even though I was shut in the conservatory, which leads into the kitchen whose door to the hall was also closed. I would not calm down and just when I had, Chris came into the kitchen en route to the boiler, and set me off again. This happened a few times; after he had left, I went round the house to confirm that he had gone and then went and weed opposite the airing cupboard where he had been working. No one knows if this was a territorial dominance thing, or whether I was just too tense to think properly. I hope he doesn't have to come back again. I don't feel comfortable with people in My house. They finally got me to bed at night time and I settled down. The next morning, we set off in the car, as is usual for a Saturday, to Sullington Warren from whence we walk home. I was in such a state that I just screamed when He drove off leaving Candy, me and Her at the Warren, and just wouldn't settle; I need everyone in my pack to be in the same place together. I fidgeted and fussed and pulled on the lead for about 40 minutes before I calmed down, but from then on, the walk was problem-free, even including encounters with cars in the lanes, though I did bark at some horses in the distance.

She said She was thinking of taking me to Doggie Day Care a couple of times a week so I can play with other dogs because part of the problem She thinks is that I'm bored. I used to run in the streets and do exactly as I liked for four years, and then I ran in the Rescue Kennels and did almost exactly as I liked there, so am finding it hard to settle down to someone else's routine. This is made worse because She can't let me off the lead until I have a better recall; there are too many roads, and worse, joggers about, which is a recipe for disaster ~ forgive the pun. I'm not a danger to other dogs, at least not yet (!) it's only people I don't trust. When Heather came to collect her newspaper this morning, I had another bout of hysterical barking, even though, again, she was a couple of rooms away from the front door. She has got in touch with a man called Mark and will discuss the problem with him when he comes on Thursday.

My capsules are back as the vet said to give them whole as the medicine inside needs the protection of the gelatine capsule to help it go down, but it does mean they get hidden in lots of pâté and soft cheese so I don't mind. It was cheese sauce today! I have forgotten my recall-on-lead, so there is no way She will let me off until I remember it again, but I'm bored with liver cake, cheese and sausage-of-any-sort so They'll have to come up with rewards that are better as I'm not responding to anything I've had before.

I have been too sleepy to write for a few days, but on Sunday, They cut down my medicine by half, so I only have one dose in the morning now, and it's much better. On Sunday, I met lots of children in the woods, and we all loved each other and I got lots of cuddles. The walk today was very new, all along the foot of the South Downs, with horses, cows, sheep and ducks, so lots to bark at; oh yes, and cars. I don't know why everyone said I was bad with traffic, I walked to Washington beside the A24 and only minded the big trucks, and then back home along the A283, ditto. If there is a grass verge (and Candy) between me and the traffic, I'm fine ~ I just panic a bit when we're on footpaths and bridleways and the cars go too fast. I got used to the horses and got tired of barking at them so stopped, but the cows mooed at me which I didn't like. She gardened this afternoon (*again*) and I barked a lot, but I think it's a bit less than before ~ not sure the neighbours would agree though.

Thursday, 21st. Six weeks here and today is my big day; I saw Mark-the-behaviourist. I had to be in my cage when he arrived, but I was there anyway as the front garden was full of tree surgeons and I didn't like the noise so thought if I barked and fought, they might go away but they didn't. And I might get out!!! He is a nice man and has a bag full of sprats, so by the time he went I was very full. I was let out of my cage and I didn't bite either him or his son Charlie, who also had treats, but meat ones not fish. She spent hours on the computer buying special new food and toys for me; Mark thinks I'm a lot more Border Collie than we first thought, so I get bored very easily and that's one reason why I bark so much in the garden, hence the new toys to keep me quiet. They're stuffed with treats too, so I will end up fat as fat! And so will Candy who obviously has to have them too, even though she doesn't do anything for them. The next day, we put into practice what Mark had suggested about joggers and horses as we went on a Downs walk with lots of both; and it worked, well, sort of. The idea is to use the treats as a distraction so I won't notice who or what is coming (fat chance of that, and what about joggers arriving round corners?) and then as a reward for being calmer. In the evening, a nice police woman arrived, and she gave me a piece of the liver cake that She had given to her; and I stopped making a fuss and relaxed, which is just what Mark recommended. I don't know how often the police are asked to feed a dangerous dog, but she had GSDs at home so understood.

Saturday, 23 March. Our long, long walk this morning was a bit of a curate's egg; coming up Chantry Lane Candy went swimming in mud so She was furious with her, and I was smug. Then a jogger came up behind and frightened us all, so I barked, but it wasn't my fault; Mark had said to give me treats before the jogger arrives so I associate joggers with food and won't bark at them but She wasn't quick enough to anticipate a jogger from behind. However, She was quick enough when it came to horses, and I was really very good because there were lots and lots of them, but I couldn't contain myself for ever and when the riders stopped to chat, I barked then. I knew She didn't really want to chat, but had to be polite. Then I saw a pheasant, and I went ballistic and barked, and barked, and barked, and barked and barked until She got really cross and made me stop, but I still kept wanting to chase it; they are very silly birds. They have just gone out for a house-warming party so I'm shut in the kitchen with Candy, but it's not bad.

On Monday, we went to our doggy day care place for the morning, and it was such fun. And no muzzle or leads! She asked the staff to check that I was all right, and that Candy was all right too, and that neither of us relied too much on the other. There were lots and lots of dogs there, a sunny place and a shady place, a sofa, outdoors, to sit on and some rugs on the ground, and a quiet room for if we were getting stressed. I can't wait to go again, and all the staff loved us. I found a real friend in a Pyrenean Mountain Dog who was huge, but very gentle. And then on Thursday, I went to Agility; Candy and I went together in the car as the weather was nice. Candy gets a bit stiff so doesn't go if it's raining or cold, but we had a lovely time except I hadn't a clue about what I was supposed to be doing. The teacher was a bit apprehensive about me at first so She kept my muzzle on, and as I was too tense to be relied on for a recall, I was on a lead too, which meant that She had to run the course with me; She was quite puffed by the end. On the way back home, She called in to a friend's for tea so we just waited in the car, and everyone who passed thought we were cute, but fortunately didn't try and stroke us.

Saturday, 30th. Oh dear, I had an upset tummy and was sick in His car, his new car, his pride and joy, as He took us all to the bottom of Chantry Lane to start our walk. *She* can't manage both directions, there and back as it's too far, so He takes us there and we walk back ~ it's still a good few miles, but a nice walk along the foot of the Downs. I do get a bit car sick anyway, but this was dreadful, and the atmosphere was toxic, a bit like my tummy. There were squirrels and men on bikes, and people running about, and cars and vans and horses and everything and I just got so worked up and hysterical I didn't know what to do; in the end I was just barking at nothing. Eventually, we got into a big field and I had diarrhoea as well. And then things calmed down a bit. Who said CBD oil worked!? I've been on it for a week or so now and it does seem to calm me down but only sometimes, and it's so much better than those tablets which just make me so sleepy. Candy went into a filthy mud puddle so She was even more fed up; I think Candy does it because she's jealous of all the attention I get. A bit further on we could see people, so stopped to chat, and the skylarks sang, and the hedgerows were full of foaming hawthorn blossom and there were tiny new lambs, and everyone calmed down and it was wonderful. I even didn't mind the horses we met, but then we crossed the gallops and just afterwards, four or five horses came galloping along making such a noise, and the ground shook, but I only sort-of barked; I was on a very, very short lead and some distance away behind a gate which was lucky. When we got back home, it was such a nice day that *They* left the doors open so I could come and go as I liked, and I barked madly again at real things and imaginary things, so I was called indoors and wouldn't come in. It was so exhausting that I slept from about 5.30 pm.

Oh dear, what another terrible beginning to the day; as we were coming back in to the utility room after our early morning wee, the heavy back door slammed on Her foot and the pain was so bad that She began to cry. I didn't know what to do so went and licked her face and hands and any bit I could find, and cuddled up to Her to make Her better, and then She cried even more. I don't think She realised until then how much I love them all, even when I'm being naughty. He took us out for a lovely quiet walk so we could all calm down and She could rest a bit, and then They had cheese for lunch so we got bits too. In the afternoon, David and Anneli came over as it was Mothering Sunday; I went into my cage with the door shut, and they both fed me liver cake through the bars, but I wanted to come out so eventually They let me out, but on a very short training lead of only about 6" so I couldn't have

34

another bite of David's bare legs. I got lots of treats though, and eventually settled down, but had to be put back before they left; She had told them that they couldn't move, get up or go to the loo while I was out as I would get upset. After they had gone, it all went quiet and relaxed again.

It's a wonder how a dog as big as I am can squash into so small a ball in the sitting room. 16 March

Chapter Three
April Showers

Sandgate Park with bluebells and the new bridge

Monday, 1 April. After a short walk, we went to Dog Day Care again, which was lovely and even better than last time. We both slept for the rest of the day, even though a someone had been in the house while we were away, I was too tired to bother. She rang Mark-the-behaviourist in the evening and I think I've got some lessons coming!

The next day, we had a lovely walk to the big field where I was supposed to be doing off-lead Recall, but the sheep were there waiting for their lambs to be born so I was kept on a lead and had my muzzle on as well... One had been born in the night and was so cute; we stood and watched it and its mother for a while and I didn't make a sound! In fact, I didn't bark at all as we walked up the road and along a wide path in woodland with primroses and anemones on either side until we came to another sheep field that the sheep had left, so I had my training there. She called me about five times and I came back each time, and got quicker doing so until the next-to-last time when I got into some really woody bits and didn't want to come out. We then walked on across another field to the stile, but someone had blocked it up and nailed the wood in place, and had secured the gate shut with too-tight baler twine which She couldn't undo, so She had to lift Candy over the stile, and then me. And I didn't mind being picked up even though I nearly got my leg stuck and after that we walked home and it was lovely and I was so good. Then, just before lunch, the phone rang and Simon (who I had nipped last time he was here) came over to discuss decorating work, so I was in my cage again and a slightly apprehensive Simon fed me liver cake so I stopped barking and let them talk. I only did a tiny bark when he got up to look around the house and then left, so I must be getting better. And we had ribs to gnaw in the garden between the showers, and came in with muddy feet! Then in the evening, something very strange happened; They were watching that big screen in the corner and there was a pheasant on it making such a noise, and the noise seemed to be all round the room so I chased round barking like mad, trying to find the bird, and then chased into the hall, but he wasn't there either. I don't understand it.

Even when I'm having a lovely time in the garden, I still chase Tanya's car up the lane on my side of the fence. She doesn't seem to mind, and when she's not in the car will stop to talk to us and even gives me a stroke through the rails; she has a little spaniel called Monty who jumps up on the rails and we sniff each other. It's fun and nice. There is another person, who drives too-fast-on-purpose, along our fence in order to make me bark and chase, and then enjoys my being told off, so She has now got two tiresome animals to deal with, which She does by ignoring the barking altogether; therefore, I rather like the tiresome girl!

Yesterday, She went off to London for the day, so it was strange not having Her there, but today is back to normal and our walk this morning was so, so long because we were looking for a suitable field to do Recall-off-lead, and they were all full of sheep. After ever such a long time, my legs got tired so I just sat down and said I wasn't going any further ~~ until I thought I saw a squirrel. And ran. I did a bit of recall training with a Wait in the kitchen and we both got treats; actually, having Candy there is quite good as she sometimes shows me what to do. Both She and I went to bed in the afternoon!

Because I had been sick in His car last week, He wouldn't take us to Sullington Warren this morning, so we walked to Sandgate Park instead; the idea is that usually on Saturdays He takes us towards Storrington and we all walk home while He pays the paper bill and runs various errands in town and drives home. We usually all get back about the same time with treats for us and coffee for Them. Sandgate Park is the "middle" area where we walk; originally, it was owned by Horsham District Council but now maintenance work is done by a team of volunteers who meet once or twice a month and cut the Rhododendron ponticum back and try and encourage the growth of the natural heathers. Within the last year, extra land has been donated by the gravel extraction firm, and hard, all-weather paths have been laid, with a crowd-funded bridge over the stream which used to be the boundary of the original park. It's a lovely area to walk with either heavy woodland with little view of the sky to wide open spaces where we watch the buzzards and I chase the ducks. There is a big pond/lake by one of the gates which is smelly and wonderful. I was let off my lead in the Park and had a lovely run. All went well for a while and then I got a scent, so like Peter Rabbit I squeezed under the gate into the sand quarry and wouldn't come back, though I did in the end and was put back on the lead. Shame! But it was a good walk because we met someone whose mother is a volunteer at the rescue kennels, and she took a photo of me to show her mother and all the staff, so I'm famous again! Not such a nice thing though was meeting a big group of runners and I went mad and barked and fought to get near to bite them, but She held my collar in one hand and had the other round my chest so I couldn't get to them, though I didn't stop barking. Some silly people decided to run right close to us instead of staying on the other side of the path, which made me even crosser. Candy was sick in the night, but we still got bones in the afternoon, as this new diet doesn't have any mixer/filler in it and we need topping up a bit. We were all in the garden after lunch and I barked and barked at the man cleaning Cyril's driveway on the other side of the lane; He was at one end of the garden by the back gate and She was round the corner at the other end in the soft fruit area, and had to keep getting up and coming round to see what all the noise was about ~ I'd follow her back to her end, and then have to go back and see what He was doing and then the barking started again. After about 1½ hours They got fed up with me and put me inside, so I continued to bark even though the blinds are kept down in the conservatory so I can't see what's going on, as it sets me off. I am exhausted!

One day, I had a lovely walk in the woods with Gill and The Gang of Agility dogs, collies and spaniels, and minimum noise. I didn't even bother to check for squirrels. When we got home, there was a Huge Van in the driveway, and a man in the house. It was Simon, who I had bitten before and he had come to decorate the dining room; well, I wasn't having that so I went mad! But they must have realised I wasn't going to like his being here because we went in the back door as usual, and all the room doors were closed so Simon was safely away from me, but I didn't like it, and let everyone know. The next day, She was out all day, so He and we sat in the conservatory all day and were very quiet while Simon worked. She had increased my drops which might have had something to do with it. I think Simon will be here for a few days; he is redecorating their bedroom and then the dining room, and is quite particular so takes quite a long time.

On Wednesday, I went to Agility, in Findon. It's meant to be Thursdays but this week it got changed, but I was sick in the car at the Findon roundabout. And again, on the way home. But Agility was wonderful and I was so good at it; we went "Over" jumps, "Through" hoops and "Turn"ed to come back again, and I learned "Weave". The trainer is still a bit scared of me because of my reputation so I had to keep my lead and muzzle on which was a shame, but perhaps next week … I was exhausted after 45 minutes, and slept all evening. It's very hard work, concentrating!

Thursday, 11 April. Another week. I arrived here on Thursday, 7 February, so this is the beginning of my 9th week, and I've found a new ploy: when no one is looking, I jump up on the comfy chair in the conservatory. I have been chased off four times today; I think they are beginning to get cross. As well as Simon, Richard the garden man also came today, so it was all a bit tense and noisy and the calming oil didn't seem to work so well today. And then She took Candy to Agility and Lyn came for His Physio so I was shut in the kitchen, conservatory, utility complex all by myself. I barked, but no one took any notice as all the doors were shut, perhaps no one heard me. Good when everyone left and we could be just us four again.

In order to keep me out of Simon's hair (or legs) and partly to meet "obstacles" i.e. runners, horses and riders, cyclists etc., we went for a long, very long walk. Not one! We saw not a soul except a little girl about my size and her brother with a bike, but the bike wasn't moving so that was all right. There was a dead rabbit on one of the lanes which I was very interested in and tried to pick up, but She wouldn't let me! She thinks I'd have eaten it, and She might have been right! The sheep and horses were too far away to be bothered with, but there were lots and lots of pheasants; as I couldn't see them but only hear them, I lost interest and we came home. However, part way up Sanctuary Lane where we had to keep going into drives to get out of the way of the traffic, someone in a Range Rover accelerated loudly just by us and I was really scared and tried to go for the car's tyres. Fortunately, we came home quickly and all sat in the conservatory to recover. In the afternoon, the television man came but I was too tired to bark, and then we had bones in the garden so I didn't care about barking at all as I had something else to think about. Just before tea time, I was given a ginger biscuit and after about half an hour taken to sit in the car; I was very scared and dribbled a lot. Then She started the engine and we drove to the end of the lane and back; I don't know why as we didn't go anywhere or do anything. We were only out about five minutes; I wonder what's going on and what will happen tomorrow?

After our walk today, Heather came in for a coffee. He has had a new idea: I might get less upset about visitors if we meet them in the Lane and then all come indoors together, so we did and Heather gave me lots of treats and it was fun and very calm. Unfortunately, she brought a friend with her, and she's afraid of dogs (so not a good idea at all and She wasn't happy, I could tell) and I did make a lunge for her but was on such a short lead, the six-inch training one, that I didn't get anywhere near her. What a pity. But it was a nice morning anyway. Bones of both sorts in the garden, and a lesson in "Hold" ~ I hated it and went to hide in my cage, even though the dumbbell I was supposed to hold was coated in La Vache Qui Rie cheese spread, which I love. We did the ginger-biscuit-car-journey thing again, but I still dribbled and was apprehensive. I wonder how long this will go on?

They've rumbled me; they now put a saucepan on the chair I like to sleep on at night when no one can see, so I can't get up there as there's not enough space left, so have to sleep in my cage. Last night wasn't funny, Candy went to bed in my cage, so I just stood and barked until She came in in her dressing gown to find out what all the noise was about, and made Candy get out. Then I had a peaceful night.

Having finished the dining room, Simon came again and this time was working outside so I had to stay indoors all day. Cross and bored, and defeated; they now put a bread board on

My chair in case the saucepan cracks one of the floor tiles if I knock it down. Tried very hard to bite the television man who came in after ringing the bell so was really wound up. Not a good walk either as too stressed to enjoy it. But a much better walk the next day in Sandgate Park and a calmer afternoon when nothing happened. Gill, whose daughter is working with dogs, told us that when a dog or a human, or any animal, gets upset, it takes up to 48 hours for the adrenaline and other hormones to settle down again, so no one is surprised that today is a Calm Day! She also invited Them to someone's house to discuss holidays because She said she couldn't invite them here because of me. HA! We also went out in the car again, and I only yawned three times and didn't dribble so much so must be getting used to it. They can't work out what I'm so scared of as I seemed all right before, but before what?

On Tuesday, I had a nice walk in Sandgate Park but the wheels fell off when we came up Sanctuary Lane as, although we tucked right into the side, this big Land Rover driven by a fat hairy man revved his engine just as he passed us so I tried to bite the car, and then was so stressed that I tried to attack two other cars that were going really slowly and carefully. Calmer afternoon when nothing happened. I now know who rules this house as there is a notice on the fence that They aren't hosting the Summer Lunch this year "because there might otherwise be leg of human on the buffet table..." so someone else is going to have to. I think She's secretly pleased that I got her off the hook!

I went to Agility this morning and did the Tunnel and Long Jump, though it was made shorter as I have such little legs. We arrived a bit early so wandered up the track and met a horse (no problems) and a big Landy (ditto) so was feeling rather pleased with myself! Agility was huge fun, though very tiring, and then Jay the trainer threw a tennis ball and I chased it round and did a Mad Maude for a few minutes, and wouldn't give it back. So, Jay, who I think knows a thing or two, threw a football into the ring and I dropped the tennis ball to chase that, but it was too big for me to pick up. So, she got the tennis ball after all; I won't fall for that one again. I didn't have a muzzle or lead on, though Jay was outside the fence in case I got a bit funny, but I wouldn't as we were not In My Garden, but in hers. Because I'm so territorial, Jay wondered whether I'd been kept or trained as a Guard Dog which might explain things. But I wasn't, though I'm not telling, so They will all have to guess. Then in the evening, Michael came; he had rung before he arrived so I was put into my crate with the door closed, but that didn't stop me from barking loud and long, and hurling myself at the bars; I wanted to bite him and send him away. After They had had a gin or two and lots of laughter, I settled down, but had to stay in my cage until They all went to bed and we were let out for a wee. Then She shut the kitchen door so I couldn't get into the rest of the house and frighten Michael.

The next day, when Michael was still here, after a play, I was put back in my cage whilst They had breakfast and I barked all over again, but wasn't quite as fierce as yesterday. During the night, I became very upset, so I took one of Her shoes into my cage; I didn't chew it, just had it by me as comforter. Then after breakfast, He, Michael, Candy and I went for a walk in the woods, and we met Gill and the Gang and Michael fussed me and it was nice, but as soon as we got back home and into our drive, I tried to attack him as I wanted him gone away from My House. I went back into my cage as

Richard was doing the garden and Robbie-the-Robot was out mowing the grass, and then after Michael went home and Richard had finished, Candy and I went to Doggy-Day-Care, and had a lovely time. We just kept awake long enough to eat the chicken feet and by then Robbie had stopped working so it was all quiet. They went out for dinner (55th wedding anniversary) so it was even quieter, until bed time then I got up onto the sofa and barked and barked at the full moon which was lighting up the garden like daylight. She came in, eventually, and I quietened down.

Today's walk was along the South Downs ~ it was a wonderful walk; skylarks singing, I ignored the pheasants as the smells were too good to miss and no runners. We met a lovely horse called JCB and I went up to him, carefully, and only sort-of barked and the woman told Her that She could walk me round her field whenever She liked so I could get more used to horses. Wasn't that nice? Then lots more horses, and cars, and bicycles and people and I almost-managed with them all, much more relaxed now Michael's gone and I have the house back to myself again. We met an eighteen-month-old dog in Sullington Warren who I tried to play with, but you can't do that on a flexi lead so I was made to stop which was a shame. Talked to Odin through his gate; I'd like to meet him properly some time. Back home, exhausted as we were out for over 2 hours; kept indoors as Robbie was working on the lawn, and I still don't like him and try to bite him, but as I've got used to Henry the Hoover, I expect I'll get used to him. Chicken feet for tea. Candy says there are suitcases in the guest room, so we expect to go back into kennels soon; I don't think they have a computer there that I can use so you won't hear much from me for a while.

We stayed there for two weeks and they collected us on Friday, 10 May; I had begun to wonder if they'd forgotten us and was almost hysterical when they arrived to take us home. SO, THEY DID COME BACK AFTER ALL!!!

Dear Dizz,

Have just sat down after putting a casserole in the slow cooker and read your very busy schedule. What I would like to know is...did you manage to nip Michael and draw blood? Because we're meeting him for lunch on Tuesday and I jokingly said I'd have the tetanus jab at the ready!! If you did I bet he was as mad as hell!

So, kennels eh? That'll be interesting for you! I suppose you can look on it as a holiday away from *Them*, a time to regroup, recharge the battery and just generally let it all hang out. You'll just be getting the hang of kennel good life when it'll be back to reality and competing with a bread board. While you're away you might want to think about how you can get the better of that hairy land rover driver – he needs to be put in his place. They think they own the roads don't they.

Bedtime for me now. Please wish *Them* Happy Hols and wish you and Candy happy hols too of course. (don't forget to pack your toothbrush and clean your teeth while you're away!)
Much love to all

Snoozie Suzie

A very relaxed little dog
April in the kitchen

Chapter Four

Maytime

The wooded part of Sandgate Park in May

Friday, 10 May. We were collected today, after such a long time, and walked home through the woods. It was strange to be back home so I had to check that everything was still in its right place.

Sunday, 19 May 2019. A slow but quiet walk and then a quiet day really until bed time when we went into the kitchen and There Was A Watery Swishing Noise, and I barked frantically. Well, She's never used the dish washer before so

I'd never heard it before, nor anything like it. But I couldn't keep that up all night, so went to bed and by morning it had stopped.

Mark-with-sprats came again and although I barked at him (I was shut in my cage), it wasn't for long and I got lots of treats when I went quiet. They talked about me a lot; She said it was sad I didn't know how to play, and Mark said that I could play, but not as domesticated English dogs did, but as Romanian street dogs did, which was mostly play-fighting. They decided that in due course I'd get the idea. After an hour or so he went, but first he had banged on the breakfast table to make a big noise, and as I didn't bark at that, he'd got up and I didn't bark at that either. Then he walked about and I didn't bark at that, but I just lost it when he knocked on the kitchen units because they reverberated and sounded different. But I soon calmed down; now, not having barked at Roger and Tanya coming home, nor at Monty going out, nor at people putting their bins out, I'm very, very full of treats and am too fat to bark at anyone. I also got done with Advocate, we both did. It must be summer again.

I learned very quickly not to stand when I could sit, and not to sit when I could lie down, so I'm having my breakfast lying down. 12 April

Knowing that treats come into my cage when I'm quiet, I stayed very quiet and wouldn't come out this morning for my cuddle or a pee, but I did come out for breakfast. I went straight back again though when we got back from the walk, just in case I got more liver cake. The next day, Richard was here when we got back from the walk, and I was quite good, and got even more treats so have decided not to move, ever. Later, She went out for the day and I went to Barking Success as Lyn was coming; when I got back, there were ribs, and no people.

We used to meet Jane and Katy in Sullington Warren on a Saturday, but today we met them in Warren Hill and had a lovely walk ~ I escaped right at the beginning as I managed to pull my extending lead out of Her hands so had a few minutes free, but the end got tangled up in some branches so She managed to catch me again. After lunch, Heather came round to teach Him how to use his mobile phone, She sat by my cage and fed me treats and I was quiet as can be even though Heather got up and walked about and She went and made coffee, and Heather was here at least an hour. So I am very good and everyone loves me! However, Robbie-the-Robot tried to steal my bone, again, and hit me, so I barked at him and he went away, but came back again a bit later and tried to steal my bone again. I don't usually mind Robbie and don't bark at him or attack him anymore, but he must learn he can't go round the garden attacking me and getting in my way, and trying to steal my bone, It's Mine. And so is the garden.

We went back to walk in "the recall field" that used to be full of in-lamb ewes but is empty now as the ewes have gone indoors at the farm to lamb. I had a lovely run around off-lead, and came back every time. Not quickly mind, I can't give Her that satisfaction ~ yet. And, when we got home, I didn't bark at loads of goings and comings round the back garden, but am very full of treats. And bones. I was brushed and heaps came out; She terrified Him by saying that there was another Dizzy in the hall made of hair!

I'm tired of being good; She was in the front garden for lots of today, so I barked at her, and anything else, and in the evening I barked at the wildebeest on television. A noisy day. And it must be Sunday because that nasty noisy dish washer was on again. The next day, we had another Recall Walk and we met two cockers that I played with off-lead in the field; I even chased a flock of geese, but they flew away. I came back each time She called, but am still not very quick about registering and doing anything about it. I do run fast though to catch up with Her as She won't chase me and just walks away. It was a better walk than a few days ago when we went, as a training exercise, to find cows, sheep, cyclists and runners, and found none of them.

It had been arranged that someone who "knew about dogs" because she'd worked with them for a few years would come round for coffee, and a discussion about my progress, but it wasn't very successful because she wouldn't listen to what She asked her to do, so instead of ignoring me until I felt calmer, she came right up to my cage And I Didn't Like It. Not one bit. So, I got all snarly and then she tried to give me treats, which I took but wished I could take her hand too. He sat in His chair by my cage, put his hand through the bars and gave me treats, but I was so anxious I couldn't settle down, and then He had to go and see the doctor so I had no comforter at my end of the room. I could sense that She was getting cross about the developing situation though She tried hard to hide it, so eventually when She'd gone to get the coffee and had insisted that the visitor sat down in a chair to wait for Her to get back from the kitchen, it all got a bit better and eventually I turned my back on them all and went to sleep; except it was only a pretend sleep as I was well aware what was going on. It didn't help that there were two deliveries with knocks on the front door and a man called about something and they chatted on the doorstep for a bit. I barked like crazy so eventually, they all went away, and then the visitor went, thank goodness, and things got back to normal; except that they didn't. The visitor had said she thought I had my wiring mixed up and that was why I was a problem; She knows a nice electrician called Roger ~ I don't think I've bitten him, yet ~ but I might be thinking of the wrong sort of wiring. The visitor also told her a bit of my background in the rescue kennels, and a bit of my history and said what a handful I had been, noisy and nipping and not really happy, but she said she didn't know how I was when all the volunteers went home at night. I might be lovely. It was a shame about today as our visitor was only doing what she thought was the best, which it wasn't.

Next day on the walk, I had my new harness on, and I hated it so I managed to wriggle out of it, and He was left with the lead and harness in His hand and no dog!!! But I didn't run away and just stood there waiting for Him to get organised and then I came back to have the lead fixed to my normal collar. Richard came but I was really good and didn't bark at him, just ignored him which was best for us both. As there was no Agility, She stayed at home so I was quiet when Lyn came, but it all got a bit tense when the delivery man came with a parcel of tea. Better later on though. I used to think this was a quiet house, but there seems to be an awful lot going on what with workmen and deliveries. And the dishwasher.

Again, we walked to try and find animals and problems but nothing except a herd of cows behind a fence; I ignored them but made a note of their smell. Long walk back through Sullington Warren and Sandgate Park where a man just appeared from behind a tree on a corner. I went for him. I was so surprised to see someone I wasn't expecting, but no harm was done as I had my muzzle on and he didn't actually seem to recognise what I had tried to do; he had his ear plugs in. Then, just after we had gone through the twitten into Vera's Walk, a woman crept up behind us in quiet sandals, and as I was surprised again, I went for her too. Had to wear my harness indoors for a bit to get used to it, but I can still get out of it!

Chapter Five

"Lazy, Hazy, Crazy Days of Summer" June

Saturday, 1 June. Back to the Recall Field and lots of fun; recall getting better. On the way home, we called into the house of the person with the two sandy-coloured cockers for a drink of water as She had forgotten to bring any, and it was boiling hot; they all talked for ages. I might like to meet them all again as the younger one wanted to play but I was on my lead so couldn't. They have a lovely garden and I think She was afraid I might destroy something. But She liked them too, so we might meet again.

The next day, it was His walk and She was meant to meet us in Warren Hill woods, for Recall training, but She forgot; He was not best pleased as He waited for ages for Her! But I was delighted because that meant I didn't have to do Training. Although I get very bored sometimes, I just don't see the point of Training.

After a lovely day yesterday when it all went calm and sunny and full of Pimms and G&T in the garden and a good lunch and bones, today was a nightmare. Michael and Freddie came for lunch; they arrived about 12.45 and I barked furiously and fretted for ages and would not settle down. After coffees in the conservatory (and I barked every time anyone moved), She served lunch so we had a bit of quiet as everyone was sat down in the kitchen where I could see Them, so felt reassured. Until Freddie got up to get a drink of water which set me off again. When lunch was over, Michael washed up so I couldn't see him and as long as he didn't speak I was all right, but She and Freddie came to sit in the conservatory and I stared at him though he didn't return my stare so I barked a lot more. Michael admitted he didn't like me, nor trust me, but then he's never been a doggy person. I didn't like his negativity and he was right that I would have had his leg off if I could have done. I couldn't decide about Freddie (one of Their grandsons) but was in such a state by then that I'd have killed anyone. When they went, after tea, it all settled down a bit but I was still upset. Why? I know I upset both Him and Her by being so very aggressive, and all for no apparent reason, particularly as I let the neighbour's car go up the lane without even a squeak at them. But in all of the noise I never heard anyone say "*Dispari!*" as I was used to hearing at home. We are all a bit upset this evening.

Gill suggested that She could turn the cage into a cave by using a blanket over the top, so I wouldn't get so upset if people came, so that's what She's done and I've been here all day. The door was open so I could have come out, but I didn't want to until it was time for ribs, and then I came out fast. And dug a hole in the central bed, again. But after last night when I went for Her as she tried to tidy my bed (from outside my cage), I didn't think it a good idea to push my luck too much.

My Cave with the blue blanket

Perhaps it was for the best that after a quiet walk today, I went to Barking Success for the day which was nice, and then Heather came for tea and although I barked at her a bit, it was a lot better than the Michael episode, though not as good as I have been.

What a day! First it was Richard who was working in the back garden; he was home when I got back so we had to go in through the front door so I didn't meet him gardening in the back, but I barked at him anyway. But not all the time, just when I could see him, so they covered my cage again with the blue blanket. Then as soon as he had gone, John and Joy came round for coffee so I barked at them too, but stopped in the end as no one was taking any notice, and my pig's ear was very tough so kept me occupied longer than usual. Lyn came early and, because it was so hot there was no Agility, again; She stayed in the conservatory with me and I was quiet until Lyn went home, but I think I barked too late because she seemed to have gone by the time, I went out to check.

I knew something was up today with all the preparations and I was right, as we had our walk (in the rain) ever so early and then She was busy in the kitchen. I was very good and didn't bark at all but Candy made up for it by racketing all the way round the woods. She was cross! David and Sandra arrived about noon for lunch which they had in the breakfast end of the kitchen, and I made a right fuss, but they ignored me so I was quiet until someone moved; Sandra wanted to go to the loo, which started me off again. They commented on what a lot of noise I made for a small dog, and I thought I'd just show them, so I did! When they went home, They put the dishwasher on again (it's been mended, sadly) so I barked at that, but not for all the time as the programme is rather long for sustained noise; it gets so tiring. Then we all went to sleep.

She has finally worked out how to put my harness on so I can't get out of it, so I wore it today but She didn't attach the lead to it, but to my collar as usual, so that I could get used to the harness first. Back to the Recall field where She has stopped calling me back so often as I just do the collie thing and check where She is and sometimes run back for a treat and sometimes just change direction so we'll meet at the end. Then we crossed into the other field and I was still off-lead so had another lovely run, but it all ended up rather messily as I found the slurry heap and ran to stand on the top of it until I smelled a dead rabbit and stared digging. I would not come back no matter how sternly, or nicely, She called; I think she was toying with the idea of climbing up after me but decided against it. When She finally caught me, I stank! So, Candy went and did the same, so she stank too. When we got home, we were shut in the garden after being hosed down, but we could all still smell the smell. After lunch, She went out and while she was away, David, Anneli and little Chloe came round; they had phoned first so I was in my cage with the door closed for safety but only barked a bit at them and then a bit more when Chloe went on MY side of the coffee table, so she walked round the room with her hands over her ears, so everyone laughed, even her. I barked a bit when David went out, but not when he came back, and a bit when Anneli went to the loo, but otherwise it was very calm. Bones in the garden in the evening.

Yesterday was lovely and quiet until bed time when I just barked and barked until about 2.30 am, and no one seemed to know why. Was it next door's security light (like the ones in Prisons) set off by wildlife, was it the wild life itself I heard, was it the wind or rain? I wish I could tell Them. This morning, He was in a very bad mood, and so was She really, but then we went out for a walk in the rain and met Henry very early on. I sat quiet while They chatted, and then suddenly She let me off the lead and I continued to just sit there. When we started walking again, I was as good as could be and we did all the walk off-lead. She didn't keep calling me back to her, just let me be and I followed where they went and caught up. I did lose Her once or twice, but she calls DizzyThisWay and I found her again. We didn't go into

Jenners Wood as it seemed too far as I have only short legs, and Candy was getting wet and tired, so we came home early but it was nice to end on a good note. Rest of the day crashed out! We had our chicken necks indoors as the rain was so heavy, and then I went back to sleep again but first I carried the tuggy into the sitting room; I'm still not sure what to do with it but I shook it about a bit pretending it was a rabbit. Or a squirrel. She bought us each a tuggy as a reward at Agility and Flyball but I only chase after it if someone throws it; what's the point of it if it just sits there? She has also taken to throwing a tennis ball about, first in the garden which made me really scared so I came in and hid in my cage, and then down the hall. Now She's getting the idea and just rolling it down the hallway and I chase it, but I don't know what to do with it then.

We're having such a busy week at the moment, there was Doggy Day Care, then when I came home, I just checked, casually like, that the visitors who I could smell, had gone. Then more visitors! My goodness! These were John and Kim from up the road; I've seen them in the lane but never got near, so I barked a bit and they looked shocked, but I soon stopped as they are lovely people and not scared or pushy or silly, so we all had a good time. And they have dogs; I could smell, and I think I've met them in the lane. I was still in my cage, but I like it there so that was all right. A day or so later, we met Jane and Katy in the woods and walked round with them, and I was off my lead and had a lovely run. This time, we went into Jenners Wood too, and I was still off-lead; I didn't want to come at the end but She caught me as I had finally found a squirrel and come to a stop. Then they decided that Jane would come round for coffee like she used to do, and

I was much better and didn't try to bite her at all, not like the other time when I did. I think She might let me out of the cage next time Jane comes round. The next day was a bit noisy as Richard was here cutting the hedges and going backwards and forwards so I barked at him, but not all the time; the blue blanket makes seeing "danger" more difficult so I'm quieter. Then She went into the back garden and Richard had left the side gate open so I ran into the front garden, did a wee, had a sniff to make sure all was right, and then came back into the back garden without even being asked. She was delighted! It made up for my escaping out of the front door this morning when Richard had just arrived and was standing on one leg by his big car changing from his driving shoes to his gardening boots and I had a little nip of his bare foot, but She called me in (I was too quick for her when I got out) and I came, though I did think twice about having a real go, but Richard had done the right thing and just stood quite still (terrified??!) so that was no fun and I came in. She was delighted by that too until She realised what I'd done, but bare feet are a temptation not to be ignored. Except Theirs, I'd never bite Them.

We went for a walk recently in Warren Hill, off-lead again, to Debbie's dismay, but she was surprised how good I was and how I didn't run away but stayed close to Her and Candy. I don't think Debbie approves of me, or indeed, of Her! I remember when Gill and Debbie were in the car park one morning as we came in, and I barked at Debbie's horse, which might be what started it all, but I think they are a lot stricter with their dogs and horses than She is with me; as She says, we can't do everything at once. But then just as we were about to come home I found a squirrel and managed to climb quite a long way off the ground up the tree trunk, but fell back

60

down into the bracken where She managed to catch me; actually, she grabbed my tail which was a bit unfair, but I didn't try and bite Her as I don't think she meant any harm. I will have to learn to be a bit quicker running away! Then They went out for a long lunch and we had bones in the garden when They got back.

However, things must be improving as I had such a busy day and I think I've ended up with 5 stars. First, we went to the Recall Field where I escaped into the neighbouring woods but as there weren't any squirrels there I came back again and ran about in the long grass. Almost as soon as we'd got home, She put me in her car and we drove to Horsham. I was supposed to be going to see the Park Run so I could get used to lots of runners, but we were too late so just wandered about the Park. There were lots and lots of people; playing football, having picnics, chasing balls, scooting on scooters and generally enjoying themselves and I didn't bark once and was so, so good. It seems that it's the determined joggers I have problems with, not children enjoying themselves. After about an hour, when all I really wanted to do was chase the ducks on the pond, we got back into the car and went off to visit Yvonne; she and her black Labrador friend Reuben write to me every now and again but I'd never met them. We went into her house and met John who isn't very well, and Yvonne gave me biscuits while She had coffee and they chatted. I was so tired I went to sleep on Y's feet; I kept my muzzle on but not my lead ~ we had started off in the garden but it was a bit boring so I came indoors to sit down. I think I might end up a PAT dog! Then we came home for a second breakfast as I hadn't had much for first breakfast in case, I was sick in the car, but I wasn't, not on either journey, so that's a plus as well.

Then there were the remains of the bones and Heather came round again; I'm getting quite used to her now and came out of my cage but spent the time trying to get the muzzle off even though Heather was feeding me sprats and biscuits. I didn't try and bite her, but was a bit edgy when she got up to leave.

Sunday, 16th. OMG!!! How can all the wheels have come off together? The walk was wet and windy and everyone was a bit fed up, but we all dried off and had coffee (Them) and biscuits (Us) and settled down. David, Anneli and William came for lunch so I was shut in my cage as Anneli had telephoned with the five-minute-warning, so it was only a bit of a bark, and I grumbled a bit when any of them got up and moved around but then I went to sleep. (The Five-Minute Warning is so that She can get me into my cage before anyone comes into the house.) When They all got up to go into the dining room, I started barking again as I didn't want to be left out so, eventually She came back in, put my muzzle on and let me out. I roared straight into the dining room and went for Anneli's leg ~ there was a lot of shouting and noise and Anneli was not pleased, so I went to rest on His feet and was quiet. I think They must have forgotten about me because ages later, at the end of the meal when David got up to get ready for going home, I chased him down the hall and went for him too. He was very, very angry and kicked me off, twice; She managed to get me away and into my cage, took my muzzle off and hid me with the blue blanket so I could calm down. David now joins Michael (his older brother) in telling Them that I need putting to sleep as I am too unpredictable, but although he was cross and used some bad language (I could tell by the tone) he didn't say *"câine nenorocit"* as people used to say at home. Whilst I miss what I was used to, this is much better, even if there's lots I still don't understand. I haven't met the two other brothers yet; I hope it's better with them. To add to everything, when David, Anneli and William had gone, She put the dishwasher on, so I barked again, and then He had his feet to close to me (again) in the sitting room so I tried to bite him, but missed. Odd about William: I didn't bark at him or take any notice of him at all and there is 6'6" of him so I could hardly fail to notice him and it was all very calm. Family tensions! During the night, I woke up at 03.40 and barked, and barked until She came in at 03.50 and I then calmed down. Went back to sleep but was very edgy all day and set Candy off barking too. Quite a quiet day but couldn't settle at night and barked until 12.50, and had refused to come indoors after our last-time wee, so stayed in the garden barking for quite a long time. What's the matter with me and why am I so upset? However, the next day I had a much better day, and it's pouring with rain so the lawn man hasn't come to upset me either. Lovely walk along the foot of the Downs, saw pigs, barked at tame ducks, didn't bark (much) at cyclist and car-that-came-much-too-close. Had ribs in the rain! Oliver had given Her a present for me; an anti-bark collar which bleeps if I bark. I had it on today for the first time and was quiet as a mouse, but IT'S NOT FAIR as it bleeps when Candy barks too, and I get the surprise.

Being a Wednesday, She went to yoga and I did Dog Pose at home and all was quiet and serene until Miles came to prune and tidy the rhododendrons and other shrubs and trees. I was kept indoors so I wouldn't bark too much and was much better than when he was here before when I had bitten him twice. We then had to give a bottle of wine to Richard to apologise for nipping him last week, but I was really good while he was here, though I had managed to wriggle out of my harness again when He took us for a walk, and then wouldn't come back and barged into a dog walker with my muzzle. He was very good and said he didn't mind, but He was cross. Lyn was here when I got back from Agility, but I was quiet until she left and then went mad. Agility wasn't very nice; I wasn't sick in the car but someone else was there with Bess and everyone seemed on edge. She knows why, but won't tell me. But here's what I've discovered, He has a name; He's called Daddy. I don't think She's got a name; I've never heard anyone use it, but She said to me "Oh go and annoy your Daddy" so I went to Him and it seems it was the right thing to do so now I know He has a name. I must try and remember it.

Today is the solstice which makes Her sad as it heralds the coming of the shorter days but it was a nice sunny day and we had a wonderful walk, off-lead for part of it, and I didn't bark at the jogger who came past because she came from behind and said Good Morning before she got to us so I knew she was there. Then we were passed by lots and lots of cars and lorries and I didn't bark, or flinch (much) at them either. I was a bit naughty when I tried to gate crash Washington School's "Indians Party" in the school field, and wouldn't come back, but I didn't eat their picnic and She caught me under the hedge in the end. When we came home, I had Recall lessons in the garden to a whistle which seems better than Her voice, and then we had bones. Went to the vet for inoculations in the afternoon, didn't wear a muzzle even though he poked and prodded me, and lifted up my tail and inserted something where I didn't think he should. I did get lots of biscuits though, because on this new raw food diet I've lost weight!

Today, being Saturday, we went to Horsham Park again for the Park Run though it was Candy that barked and barked when we got out of the car, and not me. Then, when I saw the crowds of people, I joined in, and pulled on the lead, but we both stopped after a while and She started walking us round the park. There were about 500 runners, some with dogs and some with buggies but we stood a way back and I didn't get scared once, then, as they had to run round three times, we got nearer, and then nearer still until one man, trying to avoid a loose dog, brushed my face, and I still didn't bark or get silly. I got lots of treats but really wasn't interested; the muzzle makes it so much harder to eat. Then after almost an hour or so when the runners had stopped, we walked right round the park ourselves and then got back into the car to deliver a plant to a friend; She parked in their driveway and the friend came right out to see me and got really close up and I still didn't bark, even though it was my car she was near. Then She got back in and we went to visit someone else in Horsham and She left us in the car as the friend doesn't have dogs and wouldn't like our hairs, and went in for a chat, but another visitor came with a "tiny curly dog" (no hairs) and this little dog, called Woody, jumped up at my car and I still didn't bark even though the window was wide open. Neither of us jumped out either. When we finally got home (and I wasn't sick either way), we had a second breakfast as the first one had been so tiny, and then bones in the garden and then She went out again for hours. So we three sat in the sun in the garden and had a lovely quiet time, and I didn't mind not having been off the lead as the rest of the day had been so interesting.

Today is Sunday and the dishwasher went on; I did bark at it but not as badly as at first and am getting used to it. But after a walk with Daddy (and he never lets me off the lead), I got frustrated and barked at just about everything, so when She got back from church, She gave us the holey balls with treats inside which fell into the grass and were really hard to find, so I got bored and Candy had a lot of mine. Then She tried to play ball with me; I chased it but wouldn't bring it back; I wanted her to chase me round the garden as Candy wouldn't but neither would She. So, I barked a bit more. It had been a noisy night as something had been in the garden, fox I think by the smell, so I wouldn't come in before breakfast and was all wound up and chasing this scent for most of the day. But I was better by the next day's walk to the Recall Field where I gave myself a bit of a shock as I wriggled out of the field through the stock netting that a rabbit had burrowed under, and then couldn't find my way back. She won't wait for me but just walks on and I usually know where She is and catch up, but the rabbit path went down a steep hill and I got stuck at the bottom. Got back in the end though! She's always pleased to see me even if I've been a bit naughty ~ does that mean I have the upper paw?

I had another lovely walk today off-lead for some of it ~ we went to the Recall Field but the wrong way round so I got a longer walk off-lead in all the wet grass which was taller than my tail. I did run off, but always came back (but in my time) and went back on the lead quite quietly. They went out for lunch and I chased flies in the house all afternoon. She cleaned his car in the front garden and I helped. First time in the front, and I didn't mind the people who went up and down the lane. But walking with Daddy isn't the same, as I bark at everything real or imagined, and we seem to wind each other up. She went to yoga and I went to bed and did Dog Pose.

Bones in the late afternoon. I've invented a new game; when She comes towards me with the oil dropper for my CBD oil in Her hand, I run away and hide, or bolt for my cage. She won't violate the space in my cage so then I have to get out without Her seeing, or else She chases me round the house; it's great fun, and She giggles a lot. I'm working on the same principle for when She wants to put my harness on, but not perfected that one yet.

Today, we had a startlingly quick walk without being let off the lead and straight into kennels for the day and night while They went away to a funeral. No leads or muzzles in the car to the kennels, or in the office room where we were signed in, in fact we behaved like proper trained dogs. They came back after lunch the next day and we had games in the garden and They had Pimms in the evening. As I had been good (quiet) and didn't bark much, we got lots of sausage rolls as treats. We also jumped into the car easily when She collected us but I did bark at the grooming lady as she got a bit close. The girls told Her that I also barked when people went past our kennel, but if anyone came inside that was all right and we had cuddles. Apparently, lots of dogs bark at the grooming lady; I don't know why.

Being a Saturday, it was back to Horsham Park, lots of people as before but I wasn't as shell shocked by them all, and I jumped at a man who tried to stroke me without asking first. It was very hot and Candy wanted to come home so we left early. Yvonne wasn't answering the door so we were home very, very early and just collapsed in hot heaps for the rest of the day. I had a bad hour of barking at everything that went up the lane, but then couldn't be bothered even though lots of cars went past.

2 June

Hello Tony and Ann,

It is lovely to hear that Dizzy may have met some new friends!

I don't remember saying that she has her wiring mixed up but it does appear she is suffering from past experiences and finding it difficult to shed them. Yes, Dizzy was a handful but Laura will always ensure with every dog that they are happy and if they need anything to make them happier, they always get it.

She is a very lucky girl; she couldn't be happier now! You are both very special people. V

2 June reply: Thank you for your support and encouragement ~ we will keep battling on!! She is such a love when everything goes right.

****

2 June

Have you found a publisher yet?! It's a good read!

K

****

5 June; from me, in a bit of a state, to the behaviourist:
They say that there's no such thing as a bad dog ... but oh, have I got problems. We've been married 55 years and

I'm not gong to jeopardise that for the sake of a dog, but Tony's decided that she has to go, so I'm wondering (if you think as I do that a second (thirds, fourth etc) chance would be a good idea) that you might have to come over and persuade him.

It has all kicked off following Michael and Freddie's visit on Monday; even I was a bit alarmed at the ferocity of her attacking the bars of her cage in her effort to get to him. The problem was with Michael who is a bit wary of dogs; he was the one that got bitten by Muffin a GSD who was staying with us when he was about 3 and has probably never really forgotten it, though we've had dogs for most of his life. He says he isn't afraid, but his body language tells you different. It didn't help that both are men, Freddie is 17, both are 6'4", Michael at any rate is quite a presence and the conservatory could appear a bit crowded.

Tony was severely rattled by the whole day, and that night had decided that she had "a bad streak and a screw loose, was a sick dog and had to go". I have now lost most of my back up and support and the antagonism is palpable.

Yesterday was calm and quiet and almost returned to normal: I had put a blanket over her cage to turn it into more of a cave with the added security, and she didn't really come out all day. It will be interesting to see what happens this afternoon when Heather comes round; she can cope with her and vice versa under normal circumstances.

Whether a phone call or a visit would be better I leave to you; Tony doesn't know I've written but will guess. Let me know what you decide.

Thanks for all your help; whilst I am concerned I just don't think we've reached the end of the road yet. HELP!!!!!

I am at yoga this morning, and busy for most of the day, but the evening (I know that's a bit of a cheek) is free if you want to venture then, or it can wait a day or so.

****

His reply, 5 June:

It's a shame that she is reacting to Michael, but that will be his energy, and we can't change that, only he can... you saw what she was like with me in the house, so we know she can calm down. The main thing to bear in mind is that she has improved so much with you both, and it's just the last bit that she needs help with, and that will take time and patience. She will react worse with people, who are nervous or anxious, but she will learn over time, to not react to them, but to just move away.

If it's just Michael, that she is really bad with, then I would put her into kennels when he comes over, then she can't fail, and you can all relax...

Regards,

****

12 June

Hello Tony and Ann,

So very pleased to see that your visitors are not being put off by Dizzy and her barking and if she is happy in her cage then perhaps one day, she will be more accepting.

I think the blanket is a good idea; it probably makes her feel a bit safer and it will keep her a bit cooler should the summer ever arrive!

Good luck with the mud and rain this week and see you soon.

Best wishes,

V

****

24 June

To Candy & Dizzy

Well done you two,

Don't ever give up. SHE may seem slightly odd about bedroom house rules but just ignore her. She's a bit crusty sometimes on the exterior but really quite soft underneath.

Thanks, Diz for coming for coffee and bringing Her with you. She behaved really well. You certainly have superior transport too.

And Perhaps here you didn't feel threatened, no dogs, no sudden movements...only an old lady and a sleeping partner.

As for D and M. Well I guess they don't like being charged and bitten... and they are male. That is not their fault. But it doesn't help, the human male is a strange species...and a Salmon human male quite beyond my scope of understanding. I hope that with time you will be able to accept each other.

Hope the week goes well.

Y

****

25 June, Ann wrote to Mark: Someone I met on the walk today who asked how Dizzy was getting on said, when I had told her about the Fun Runners in Horsham Park on Saturday, that she wasn't being good at all but was just completely shell shocked and was incapable of reacting.

Was she right? Did I do the right thing by trying to get her desensitised to runners or did I just make a bad situation worse? We haven't met any local runners since Saturday, so I don't know how she would behave now.

Would love to know what to do now as I had intended to go to Horsham park again this Saturday

Ann

25 June, From Mark:

Re: her behaviour during and after the Park Run; There is certainly an argument to say that she simply shut down as she couldn't handle that amount of people, but then I would have expected her to react more in the car. Trigger stacking will play a huge part in that day as she would have had to put up with lots of runners. You haven't made her worse, but I wouldn't take her to a really busy place as that may be too much, I would still go to the park, but not when there are too many dogs, people and runners etc.

The other experiences that day sounds like she did really well.

Regards, Mark

****

On 23 June 2019, I wrote to Sue:

We aren't supposed to go into the bedrooms, but this is "the collie creep" and I think we got away with it!

Sweet dreams!! (Pictures inserted.)

Dear Dizzy,

Well I think ***Congratulations*** are in order on your 6-month survival! That's incredible how those 6/12 have flown by, and by the sounds of things there's not been a dull moment except perhaps when you pop into your cage/ sanctuary for a bit of peace and quiet. There's a lovely photo of you in the cage looking very content and dare I say it – a tad pleased with yourself! So, thanks for sending that on. It also sounds as though you're gaining a huge amount of confidence which is great – well done you! Mind you, you are extremely fortunate that *Her* and *Him* are able to give you so much time and all those lovely long walks and activities.

So glad you're enjoying life.

Love to all

Sue xx

Candy and me at the bedroom door; we aren't supposed to go into the bedrooms, but this is "the collie creep" and I think we got away with it!

Chapter Six
Glorious Summer Days in July

Monday, 1 July 2019. I've had such fun and been so naughty, but as She's never really cross it doesn't matter. First, we walked to the big field in Washington, negotiated the stile with all the stock netting round it and I was let off the lead. Candy and I ran and ran as She began to head towards the other stile to leave the field. Well, I wasn't going yet so ran off along the field side of the A24 to see if I could find squirrels or rabbits, and ignored her calling me; then She turned the other way back to the first stile so I decided to come too. But not close enough to be caught. Then I found I could wriggle through the stile as the netting had been removed since last week and chased into the wood yard which smelled such fun, and I wouldn't come back. When eventually I was caught, I stank like Candy does sometimes, and my harness was full of weed seeds and mud. I was a bit subdued after that and didn't bark at the cyclist, though he had stopped on the path to let us pass, and went into my cage when we got home. The next day, I was kept on the lead for all the walk and was very frustrated. Jane came round for coffee and I was let out of the cage, eventually, as I had been so good before, and everything was wonderful, and I was without my muzzle. Jane sat still and had her special tea, while She had coffee, and it was like this for a long time. I got lots of treats and cuddles, and then Jane stood up and I went for her, but immediately after I screamed ~ it was an awful noise and neither Jane nor She had ever heard anything like it. I was hustled unceremoniously back into my cage. After She had applied TCP and dressed the bite, they walked to the door and stood there talking for a while about the noise I made; they decided it was as if I was being kicked myself, that sort of a noise. They surmised that that must have been what used to happen, if I bit to defend my space, the person would kick me hard to get me away, and I screamed. Am now bored with lots of energy and nothing to do and shut in my cage to calm down. After lunch, She decorated a birthday cake and won't even let us lick out the bowl, but we did get ribs again.

Wednesday. She took us out as Daddy wasn't very well and then dashed off somewhere, so we had a quiet day until Heather and Tricia came round, but I didn't bark very much at all and Heather gave me treats and patted me through the bars of the cage. I think if Tricia hadn't been here, She might have let me out as I like Heather. I also took the tennis ball into the sitting room and then into my cage, and I took a tuggy as well. Perhaps I will learn to play.

Daddy was better the next day though, so he took us out, but very slowly and when we got back, the drive was full of vans; the man had come to put the new carpet down in the dining room, but as the kitchen door was closed I never got to see him or bite him. While She was talking to him, I had a bit of a bark, but Daddy sat in the conservatory with me and kept me quiet. Then he went away but Richard was still here in the garden, but I don't bark at him as much now unless he gets too close to the conservatory windows. Then he went away as well and I went into the dining room and peed on the carpet to make sure everyone knew it was my carpet in my house. Daddy was beyond speechless, but She just mopped it up and although I can see where it was, and I think She can too, no one else can. In the afternoon we went to Agility, and met Heather and Tricia with Bess. I really didn't want to do Agility, or perhaps I've just forgotten what to do as it's been a bit on/off these last few weeks since They went away for such a long time, and then it was hot, so I wasn't very good at it. When we got home, She shut us both in the kitchen and went out again, but as I couldn't see Lyn I didn't bark until she left (when I could see her through the kitchen door) and then we had ribs in the garden. In the evening, someone called Rhia came; she remembered Candy and all the other dogs from long ago and she sat in a chair and after a few minutes I stopped barking and lay quietly. Not asleep mind, but pretending. I let her feed me treats and sprats through the bars and was really gentle until she fed Candy too, and then I got jealous and furious, but it all fizzled out very soon. When she went home, I didn't bark at her until she was in the hall with the front door open; I hope she comes again as she's nice, and very calming. She knows about dogs.

Today, I've found a friend! And we played for ages and ages and I was so good and did all the right things, that I've got a halo. We drove down to the Bluebird Cafe and met Jane and Katy and went for a walk along the beach; at first, I thought it might be boring as I was still on the grass and therefore on the lead, but that was because there were horses cantering along on the sand. When we'd passed the horses, She let me off and I ran into the bushes, but never too far away, and then Katy met a little friend so I just came back as they were all standing still, and lay down. We walked on the grass for a long way and then changed direction to the sea, and Katy went in to play with me and we chased each other in and out of the water and up and down the beach until I saw Something in the water and barked at it, but it didn't move, so I left it. I chased gulls, and a jogger but didn't get too near and just barked at him and came back to everyone almost at once, and then there was a man on a bike so I chased across the beach to chase him, but came back again and didn't try and bite anyone. There were a few children on the beach too, but I didn't bother with them. Katy and I just played for ages and ages. I got soaked and so did Candy who was hot so she just lay down in the sea, but by the time we got home we'd both dried off. I got lots of treats as I kept coming back and wasn't trying to bite or head butt anyone, and a huge drink of water by the car. So hot I couldn't settle when we got home but cooled down and slept most of the afternoon. Whilst in the garden, I barked like mad at Caroline, Andrew and Coco who came past, but didn't bark at all at Tanya, Roger and Monty who were also going for a walk, so must be very confused ~~ I know She is! It was a lovely day and I hope we do it again as I like Katy. Jane also had a suggestion for Her, that She put my blankets in the dining room so that it smells of me and not new carpet and the carpet man and, therefore, I won't be naughty again as the room will smell of me.

Today, it is Washington Village Fair so we went on a shortish walk first to Sandgate Park where I was let off the lead and disappeared into the bushes after a squirrel, but came back within about four minutes. Happy to go back on the lead as I had had my fun. In the afternoon, we went to the Fair and I saw lots of little children running about and stalls, and a band

and didn't mind at all; then we went to see the donkey who was standing in the shade in a corner of the field. He didn't seem to mind me either, even though I had given a warning bark at the beginning, but the donkey man was very tense and tiresome; She wanted me to stay still and get the scent and idea of the donkey who I'd not met before, but he kept moving between the donkey and me so I never got a good look. Then he got cross with Her (never a good idea) after She had explained that I'd not seen a donkey before and this was part of a training exercise, and he said that She had no business training her dog in a public field … and She then began a reply but he was so aggressive that I got scared and started to bark, so we left him and went to see the Birds of Prey instead. I didn't mind at first but I didn't like them flying so close to me and wanted to chase them so just barked at them instead, so She got up off the grass and we came home, after going round again for a bit to calm down. It was very hot so they had tea and then drinks in the garden in the shade and Candy and I stayed beside them. Then tennis on television and bed.

A bad day that just got worse. I didn't want to come out of my bed to do a morning wee, and I didn't want a morning cuddle either. I came out for breakfast and a very slow walk, then back until Andrew and Tracey came for lunch; they came straight into the conservatory where I was safely in my cage and sat down just as She had told them to, and I barked at them a bit, but only for a minute or so. Then it was all happy and Andrew fed me sprats and treats and petted me through the bars and I liked him, but Tracey was a bit nervous so I barked at her when she stood up, so she became even more nervous. When everyone went into the dining room for lunch, She came and put my muzzle on (after the Anneli event) and

I sat under Daddy's chair. After a few glasses of wine, I think everyone had forgotten about me again, because at the end of the meal they all got up and I managed to bite Tracey even though I had my muzzle on. It wasn't a bad nip, and she was very good and didn't make a fuss, but I shouldn't have done it. They went home soon after that. That night, there was Something In The Garden so I barked all night; by 4.30 even She was cross, and I was tired and it was daylight so I shut up. Then a lot of barking at first on the walk. Eventually, we all calmed down and it was a quiet day. Tuesday was another noisy night then a quiet day after a bit of barking on the walk and a general twitchiness for every sound. I don't know why but I remained on edge and stressed for the next couple of days.

After about four days I had a quiet night and felt a bit less stressed which is a good thing as Richard is here. I don't bark at him much nowadays, but I still do a bit. I don't like it when She shuts the kitchen door even if I'm in the conservatory with Daddy, or anyone else for that matter, I like all the doors open so I have an escape route. I wouldn't come into the house this morning after She went out to empty the compost bucket into the compost bin; with returning self-confidence I'm trying it on somewhat. We also had a visit from Tim the lawn man who I barked at ferociously until Daddy calmed me down and got me off the conservatory sofa where I had had the vantage point of being able to see into all the back garden and see what Tim was up to; Tim was here about 20 minutes so it was a long time to be quiet. In the afternoon, I went to Agility and did quite well until I got tired, and I played with a ball too, and then we came home and just as the tea was poured we had Kim and John for a "be barked at" session and they said how much better I was since last time, and I let them feed me sprats. Perhaps visitors are nice after all.

I had a nice walk on the Downs today, but still on the lead after all the tensions of the week. It was very hot so we stayed quiet most of the day and just went out for our bones. I also let Roger and Tanya drive to work without barking at them, and I ignored the postman's van. It was too hot and exhausting to do anything else.

It is a week now since The Donkey Man upset us both and I've now remembered about Recall, which I'd forgotten for the whole of the week. I'd also forgotten just about everything else too which may explain why I've been on the lead such a lot. Today, we went to Sullington Warren and She let me off the lead and I ran round in the flowers and came back both times She called, then I went back on the lead for a bit and was let off again, and came back again. So, we're all happy and I'm puffed out. I barked at people in the lane, but not as much as I usually do, and that may be because She has cut back lots of the flowers that were obscuring my view of the lane, and I can now see everything! Daddy kicked me again; he really has big feet and doesn't seem to know where they are, which he ought to as my head is usually on one of them; perhaps that's the problem? But when we go into the sitting room to watch television, or into the conservatory for coffee, I have to put my head somewhere and his feet are comforting and comfy. I also like to rest with my head up; it's an old habit and gives me a split second of advantage if I have to run away from danger, so even though this house doesn't have any danger, it's a habit I won't let go of. Yet.

As it's Sunday today, we had a quiet-ish walk with Daddy ~ however, there is one place where I am sure the squirrels live so I bark there when going in either direction, but it was hot and humid and we all got tired very quickly so came home. No visitors, and very little barking at people in the lane, and I didn't even bother with the dishwasher. But I pulled a lot on the lead so now his shoulder hurts. And I barked at people taking out the bins. I do not like wheely bins.

The sheep seem to have come back into The Recall Field; they didn't bother me, but one group chased Candy, and there was me thinking she was the sheep dog, not the chased-by-sheep dog. Lovely free run in another field though, and a long bark with Odin at the end of the lane. Mrs Odin might be coming to see me and "be barked at with the reward of coffee and a chocolate biscuit" some time in a week or two. Had another spat with Candy as she got too close in the sitting room, which is silly as we practically sleep together during the days when it's cooler. She gardened for a while and I didn't bark at Roger, Tanya and Monty either when they went out or came home, though I did bark at The Neighbour I Don't Like, and He Doesn't Like Me in return and at Cyril's wheelie bin.

They don't seem to realise that we know what they're thinking! Because even though today was another quiet day, my friend Laura was meant to come and see me but she didn't, probably busy. But Candy knew Something Was Up so she kept rushing to the front door barking, and I had to be hustled into my cage, also barking, and there was never anyone at the front door after all. This happened about three times, until They had decided that it was too late for Laura to come, so they made another pot of tea and everything calmed down. You see, we're cleverer than they thought!

Today was a very curate's-eggy day, first I was very good and ignored the horses we passed on the walk, and then She put me on the new very long lead which was quite fun but I didn't go dashing off into the cornfield and did do quite good Recalls (but still in my own time.) But then I went under the gate and when She called me back, I went a different way and got the lead all tied up round the gatepost, so She had to come and untangle me which made Her very cross as it had rained in the night and the lead was wet and sandy. Her trousers were already sopping from the long grass so She was easily upset. Then in Sanctuary Lane, there was a problem with two big vans trying to get past each other and failing, and the traffic built up behind them and I got very scared and tried to attack one of the vans, and then the other one, and then a third which arrived so I was in a bit of a state when we finally got home. There was Agility in the afternoon; I don't have my muzzle on which is good, but I just didn't see the point and was very otherwise, until She rolled me over and tickled my tummy and I thought it was a game and was galvanised into action. It didn't last long, because my idea of a game was the street play-biting games, and every time I tried to nip her leg, She said NO and made me jump over the bar; so I lost interest. But the good bit was good. Rhia came round in the evening to "be barked at" which was nice as I didn't bark at her much or for very long, and went to sleep. I did bark when she left though as I hadn't expected her to move!

We had a very noisy walk in the woods today, and some Recall training on the long lead which was hitched to a log seat, then home for Bones. Someone called Zoe arrived at tea time and has come to stay, so I barked a lot, but did calm down eventually, and stopped entirely after tea, until she got up to go to the loo, which started me off again. However, by supper time I was quiet, though still locked into my cage, so She and Zoe went into the sitting room and Daddy took us into the garden for a pee and a run around. Well, we ran, he didn't. When Zoe went to bed, she took her glass of water with her so she didn't have to come into the kitchen because we had the run of the kitchen, utility and conservatory. Zoe was told not to come in until we had been let out for a pee in the morning, and She had taken in a cup of early morning tea for her when I was back in my cage and everything was safe.

Saturday started so well; She had even decided that after our walk I could come out of my cage as I was getting on so well with Zoe. After breakfast, it was arranged that Zoe would get her boots out of the car and walk towards the shelter at the end of the lane, so we could meet in "neutral territory" as I had been shut in my cage all the time she was in the house. She checked that Zoe had gone; not in the bedroom, not in the loo, not in the house, so She opened the kitchen door so I could run round a bit until I got my harness on, and then, for some inexplicable reason Zoe forgot the rules and opened the front door to put her car keys on the window sill. Well, that was a red rag to my bull, so, as I was in the hall anyway, I charged through the open front door and bit her leg, hard. She screamed, went to pieces and all hell broke loose. I was hustled back into the kitchen, Zoe was plied with TCP and dressings, and at that moment Daddy came back from the newsagents to this chaos. She was furious, and for once, not with me! We set off for the walk as arranged last night, and Zoe tagged along behind us but both Zoe and I were in such a state that I barked and fussed until Zoe decided that as I now viewed her as an intruder, she'd better go back home. Which was a relief to us all. But then I just couldn't face a walk and sat down in the car park and wouldn't move, until She asked me where I wanted to go and She followed me, but we were not out for more than ¾ hour and I barked at squirrels, real and imaginary, all the time. It was all very stressful. I had to go straight into my cage with the door shut (Zoe was hiding in the sitting room) but she was so scared that she sat in the conservatory with her coffee in a blue funk while I barked at her and the situation began to turn in ever noisier downward circles. Eventually, They all had lunch and I couldn't see Zoe so I lay down and tried to relax, but every time she spoke, and she talks a lot, it set me off barking again. In the afternoon, Zoe and She went into the garden to do some work, and Daddy stayed beside my cage in the conservatory to keep me calm, but it was a real battle; I calmed down a bit after tea, but it was a horrid day. It didn't really get better even though Zoe and She were shut in the sitting room and Candy and I were shut outdoors, but I did do a lot of racing round the garden. Let us hope Zoe goes soon and life can calm down again; she gets me in such a state.

The next day, Daddy took us out before Zoe got up, and when we got back, she and She were having coffee in the garden, so our paths didn't cross until nearly lunch time; when I barked very hard. She had thought that Zoe and I would be calmer after a night's sleep but she wasn't and threatened to go home, and then She got really cross ~ with everyone; She shouted at me to Shut Up, and said the same to Zoe, told us both to pull ourselves together and behave like sensible grownups. So, I stopped barking and Zoe had lunch and a glass of wine, and things settled down. She did go home just before tea time, so we settled down to golf on the telly and quiet, but I was still very stressed and panting a lot. Hope we have a quiet night, tonight.

The Monday after the weekend before ~ *after a lot of thought and a "sleep-on-it" ~ we are recovering from the weekend of high tension, and have had a calm and peaceful day with a good long walk to calm nerves, the back door open and easy access to ribs in the garden. The morning walk was interesting, Dizzy barked at heavy traffic (something she hasn't done for weeks) and at the pigs, which she hasn't done either, but on the plus side, she was very relaxed when we met three horses, even when one, having passed us, decided to turn round and prance back the way it had come, towards us. A cyclist on the road was so quiet he made both Dizzy and me jump, so I wasn't surprised at her reaction. More interesting though was that Candy didn't once have her tail in "collie mode"; carried low, tip curled up and waving from side to side as she walked ~ it was up like a scorpion's tail, very tense. All is better this evening though and I'm hoping for a fairly calm day tomorrow too, so that by Wednesday we might be back on an even keel. I have had thoughts about how we (I) handled the situation and I still feel that I did everything to make life safe for Zoe, and that it was her extreme fear and anxiety which made Dizzy worse, which made her worse too, so we were on an ever-increasingly descending circle. When we were having coffee in the garden yesterday morning, Zoe was in a real twitter imagining opening doors heralding Tony and the dogs' return even though they go out for a good hour plus, and had only been gone about 15 minutes. I think if any of my trees had been old enough to climb, she'd have climbed one "to be safe". She kept asking if the cage was safe, and whether its door was shut, but I still think I did the right thing in making her stay for lunch (propelled into the conservatory with a packet of frozen peas which I happened to have in my hand at the time) and have a glass of wine (it was that sort of time) because if she had left at that moment, a) Dizzy would have accomplished her objective of barking her into submission, and b) Zoe would have kicked herself for the rest of time for 'chickening out'. The bite is clean and uninfected and I hope will heal well. I just hope that our friendship will heal too.*

The next day, They went away for the day, so after a quiet-ish walk we went to Doggie Day Care for the day. I did get a bit worried and barked with my paws up the fence as She left us, and a bit more worried when They took so long to come and collect us again, but it was all right in the end. Then, goodness, what a night; Candy was so scared of the thunder and lightning that she went into Their bedroom, and was allowed to stay, but I waited in the doorway, and then went back into my bed, but She came and sat on the floor beside me as I didn't have Candy for company. In the morning, Daddy took us for our walk, but it was very, very hot and humid even though it was so early, and we were all hot and tired, so came home early and we lay on the stone floor all day to get cool. Heather came in the late afternoon and although I barked a bit, I soon stopped and was let out of the cage (with my muzzle on and the very short lead) to see her; I rubbed my face against her trousers to get the muzzle off, but failed. However, she did give me lots of sprats. Then I barked a bit as a neighbour took his wheelie bin back up the lane, but stopped when She came to be beside me and Heather left without any noise from me at all! Lots of gold stars, for Heather and me. Perhaps things are getting calmer, for all of us. Because of the extreme heat Agility was cancelled, so I was here when Lyn came but I didn't bark at her, nor when she left. They had supper and a bottle of wine in the garden when things cooled down a bit and I spent a happy evening rummaging in the flower beds, and barking at Cyril who was shutting his sitting room windows. That night, we had yet another stormy night with lightning and thunder so we both went into Their bedroom for comfort. A few days later, Laura from the rescue kennels where I lived came to see me and it was wonderful; I hadn't forgotten her at all, and I was let out of the cage at once, without a muzzle and we had such a cuddle and play and treats and I got really excited. It was a lovely end to a lovely day. Laura told Them lots of stories about me and what I had done, and the two other homes I had gone to but had to be returned, so She was very interested.

Saturday, 27th. We were very good and didn't go into Their bedroom as it wasn't stormy; I think we're only allowed in when there's thunder and lightning. We had a lovely walk, off-lead all round Sullington Warren and Sandgate Park, and I only went back on the lead when we'd crossed the new bridge. Candy went into the lake to get really wet, but we were all pretty wet as it didn't stop raining all walk. I had such fun chasing scents and exploring, and was tired out when we got home, so have spent much of the time back in my cage. It was funny because I didn't want to get up this morning and only came out for my breakfast (of sprats) and then went straight back, She said that She wasn't going to give me breakfast in bed so I'd have to get up. It seems to be shaping up for another lovely day. Fingers crossed!

On Sunday, we made history; all four of us went for a walk today in Warren Hill and Jenners Wood. For some reason, They never go out together; I think it's because we behave so differently with each of them that They are afraid we will be confused as to who is in charge ~ well, that's easy, it's ME. We were out for about 1½ hours and I was off-lead all the time; it was wonderful. I barked a lot at squirrels, real and imaginary, and just ran everywhere; but I kept checking that they were about and got lots of cuddles when I did, and I came back at the end to have my lead put on. When we all got home, we were all so exhausted They had coffee and we slept on the cool tiled floor.

Next day, after a walk off lead in Warren Hill woods, we went on to our day care at Barking Success for the day. When we were collected, the house smelled different, and Simon (who is scared of me because months ago I bit him) was decorating the kitchen and utility room, and the conservatory doors, so we had to be kept out of his way, and spent the rest of the afternoon in the sitting room. The next day, after Daddy had taken us out to Warren Hill and let me off-lead, we came back and I found my cage had moved into the sitting room, where we were all incarcerated for the rest of the day until Simon went home. She came home at tea time. On Wednesday, I had my first breakfast of mange tout and asparagus poached in butter; the doggy bag from Their lunch yesterday when They went out with friends, again!

****

8 July. Email from Her to Andrew about yesterday

I hope Tracey is all right after the dramas of yesterday. Whilst I am sorry about the nip, I am more sorry that the event might have reduced her self-confidence with dogs, so I hope the relationship with Murphy won't be jeopardised.

I had no idea that the muzzle wasn't the total deterrent that I had thought it was, and it was doubly a shame as you and Diz were getting on so well.

I am really, really sorry, and am sure that when we meet again on neutral ground there will be no repetition.

Andrew's reply a few days later:

No worries about Dizzy or dogs in general. That is why Tracey wanted to speak to you personally when we got back home, to reassure you. On reflection, things happened very quickly and there were a number of lunges from Diz, each of which may have caught a single tooth rather than 1 actual bite. That might explain how Tracey was caught and the muzzle may still be working as expected.

Regards, Andrew

9 July. Letter to Mark the behaviourist, and his replies:

So, following various nipping episodes in the dining room, the questions are:

· **Is it meals in the dining room ~ we only eat there when family come on a Sunday as the kitchen table is too small?**

A. Location may play a part as it's not the usual place for her. Try using the dining room more often.

· **Is it just too many people all at once, even though the maximum has been 5?**

A. Quite possibly, she will be upset by lots of people.

· **Is it too much excitement the day before, though we were only at the Fair about half an hour? Particularly after what you'd said before about overload.**

A. Again, quite possibly, she will want to relax at home quietly.

· **Anneli and Tracey sat in exactly the same place round the table ~ is it the chair position?**

A. Not likely.

· **I don't think it can be the small of food; we have a Sunday roast each week.**

A. No it won't be that.

· **I don't think it can be the smell of alcohol (though I know wolves don't like it) as we have a G&T/Pimms/bottle of red most Sundays.**

A. No it won't be that.

· **How can she nip through a muzzle?**

A. Very easily, I have been nipped a few times through a muzzle, they just can't bite properly.

· **What am I missing?**

A. Not so much missing, rather than putting her into situations where she is going to struggle. I would be inclined to put her into Old Clayton when you have lots of people over, or at least in a completely separate room with brain draining activities. Then she can't fail. Our focus always fails when we have to entertain others.

Regards,

****

28 July

Hello Ann,

I was absolutely delighted to read about Laura's visit. I'm not at all surprised that Dizzy remembered her – all the dogs react in the same way when they see Laura. How lovely for Dizzy to have such a special visitor!

I shall look forward to hearing all about Laura's visit when we have our beach walk on the 5th. It will be low tide so our girls can have a lovely run and play together. Katie will be so pleased to see you all, but especially Dizzy.

Jane

****

Chapter Seven

August

Thursday, 1 August 2019. What a chaotic day; first Daddy took us out early to get out before Simon came, and I ran off-lead again. When we got home, we were taken into the sitting room, where She was, for coffee and our water, so that we wouldn't be in Simon's way. When He went to the doctor, I was a real nuisance as I barked and whined and grizzled the whole time He was out. And then I attacked the woodwork round the door glass. As soon as He came back, She went to the dentist, and I behaved much better; lunch was on a tray in the sitting room as we still can't go into the kitchen, and then Richard arrived to park his vehicle in our driveway as his new customer hasn't got space, and I barked at him. Then She and I went to Agility, Candy is getting a bit old and stiff to come any more. I was brilliant; we've had a few weeks when I didn't see the point of Agility and wouldn't do it, and if anyone tried to make me I lay down and wouldn't budge, but today I got brownie points and liver cake. As Jay had suggested we had had a much shorter walk so I had more energy too. I mastered the Dog Walk, including the 'wait' at the centre, and the touch points, and jumped all the jumps, and killed my tuggy when She threw it for me, which was a good reward. We went off to buy some paint after Agility, and then went to the beach for a bit until She had estimated that Lyn and Richard and Simon had all gone home. When we got back, Candy told me that she helped Lyn with the Pilates exercises as the sitting room door was open and she went in, but was very quiet and good (she said!) When we finally got home, I went into my cage to sleep. In the evening, the cage went back into the conservatory where it belongs and things got a bit back to normal, which was nice.

I did say things might be getting back to normal, well, on a long walk, with some of it off-lead, I went off exploring and got stuck on the other side of the river and couldn't get back, but She won't wait for me so I really had to work out how to catch them up. Candy had run in a muddy ditch earlier on, and after my escapade I was filthy too, but by the time we got home most of it had dried, though we both smelled pretty awful. We met one cyclist on a wide bridleway, and he wouldn't move to the other side of the road to give me space, so I got a bit agitated, but am a lot better than I used to be. No painters, no vans, no nothing to bark at, so I barked at the pigeons instead. We had bones in the garden, and I began to settle down a bit. Normal, at last!

Today was a Saturday so we went in the car to Sullington Warren where I was let off-lead, but decided I wasn't going to do Recall; I had to change my mind a bit when She started walking the other way and I had to run to catch up. She caught me and I went back on the extending lead, but I do Recall very well in those circumstances, so She let me off again but attached to a running lead; all was well until She went the wrong way and had to turn back, but I was too far ahead to realise. After a while, I managed to locate more or less where they were, and was running back to them when my running lead got caught in a tree root and I was stuck. I could hear Her calling and didn't know what to do, so I barked instead, and She managed to find me; I was relieved. I came home on the Flexi after that, but was in a bit of a state and barked at a car. Heather and Tricia came round for coffee and I didn't bark at them, even when Tricia stood up and started walking round the conservatory; they were here for about 1½ hours and I didn't fuss at all, even when they went to the front door to go. Lots of sprats and cuddles and Brownie points, and yesterday's bones in the garden. The next day, Daddy took us out and he can't manage the running lead as it's too long and cumbersome, so I was off-lead and having fun. We met a man on a mobility scooter with his black lab riding in the footwell and I wasn't scared of him, and then a cyclist came up behind us, no one had heard him, and I didn't mind him either, and he said thank you as he passed. I got very dirty feet in Jenners Wood but it didn't seem to matter. When we got home, I barked at Cyril, but then I always do.

Monday, 5 August 2019. "I am exemplary!" She said so. We had to drive to our walk today and I felt very nauseated, yawning and dribbling in the car until we arrived at the beach, meeting Jane and Katy at the Bluebird Cafe in a fine drizzle that got wetter by the minute. When we got to the cafe and away from the car park, I was off-lead, and pottered along the greensward having fun by myself. Then Katy and I played chase, and then we played chase with other dogs too and it was all lovely even if it was pouring, wet and windy by then. Two men came running towards us, a fat white one and a thin black one, and when She asked them to stop or walk past us, they just ignored Her, so I went to bark at them, but didn't go to bite. I soon stopped and ran on to do other things, and then, would you believe it, the same men turned round and ran back towards us again. She said they did it on purpose just to annoy us; I had a very small bark but nothing really. Then after a bit they stopped in front of us and started doing some exercises, sitting on the ground, so just to prove Her point, I walked past them totally ignoring them because they weren't running. We then came off the grass and across the sand and Katy jumped over the groynes but my legs are too short so I had to run round the end of them, but I did manage to jump through one set of them, to huge praise from Them. Katy and I chased for another hour as we walked back to the cafe, and the sun came out and everyone began to dry off a bit. Jane invited us all back for coffee and lunch, so we drove a short way to her house and went to play in the garden and have a drink of water in the kitchen. Jane said Katy was a bit particular about who she let into her house, so we were all very privileged that we were allowed in, first to the kitchen, then to the dining area, and finally to the sitting area where They had scones and tea. I don't quite understand what happened next, but suddenly Katy jumped up from her place on the sofa and snarled and bared her teeth at me, and I shot backwards out of harm's way. Then she settled down again as if nothing had happened. And then she did it again; Jane was always very quick to defuse the situation but I was beginning to get a bit apprehensive, so after the third time we all went out for a walk to the local park, to cool off a bit. It also meant that when we walked back to our car, we didn't go in the house again so we left on a happy note. When we got home, Simon was still here but clearing up and left soon after so I didn't have to see him and upset him, then we had ribs in the garden and a quiet evening. At the bedtime pee though, I managed to bark so loud and long that I probably woke everyone in the county up. She said I was just letting off steam, but I'm not sure where the steam came from.

This morning, the refuse bin was upended and the contents were all over the garden; I did tell them it was foxes as I'd barked all night. Went out for as long a walk as possible while Simon finished off; met a nice Australian couple who were missing their dogs and as Candy didn't want to be fussed, I stood in instead. Then I got bored and chased imaginary squirrels, but they were still talking, so I chased off again and came back again, and eventually we went on our way. A lovely peaceful afternoon with no workmen or anything, but Candy was very fretful so I got noisy as well.

Wednesday, 7 August. My six-month birthday here! I was good on my walk with Daddy to celebrate but barked a bit at Tanya as it was bin day and I don't like the noise. She stopped and talked to me, so I stopped barking, and then came indoors. Ribs in the sunny garden and a nice quiet day, until the man came to take the broken television away as he couldn't mend it here. Then They had to spend the evening in the conservatory as it is the only room with the other television, and it's too small to put in the sitting room where the big one was. It and I were all disorganised. After that things just seemed to get worse, as She had had to bring her lace pillow and lamp and paraphernalia into the conservatory so She could make lace while watching the news and other programmes in the evening. It had all gone wrong and upset, and I was very fretful and barked at Richard, the post man, delivery vans, activity at Cyril's house and anything else I could think of; Daddy got cross and irritable and I got worse. Next day, we went to Agility, but I had walked in the morning so I was too exhausted to do anything properly and I fell off the dog walk. Not good really, but not quite back to square one. Then that night, the wind was dreadful and Candy was so worried she went into Their bedroom for comfort, and I hid at the back of my cage. Not happy.

The next day, our walk started at Sullington Warren but it was so scary with the trees blowing and the branches so low that I lay down and wouldn't go any further so She picked me up and carried me through the nasty bits to the open space where I was better. I played with a huge mountain dog, but he got very boisterous chasing me, so I squeaked, and when I got between Her knees again, She put me back on the lead which was comforting. Then I chased into a hawthorn thicket and didn't come out the way I'd gone in so She got very scratched untangling the extending lead I was on; the wind got worse and we met a couple with the husband holding tight to his wife who had been blown over so I was glad to get home. As it was Saturday, Heather came to collect her paper and I came out of my cage and was very good (and very demanding) having my tummy tickled while she tried to explain to Daddy all about how to sort out his His iPhone problems; she was walking about in the conservatory and I didn't mind at all. Then, she'd stayed so long that They invited her to stay for lunch (cheese on toast so we both got a bit of cheese as a treat) which they ate off a tray in the conservatory and I was still good. I didn't bark when Heather got up to go home a few hours later, I think she's part of the family now. I didn't even bark at cars in the lane, so must be becoming a Reformed Character. A Good Day and lots of sprats! Meals were a bit odd as we only had a tiny breakfast in case I was sick in Daddy's car on the way to Sullington Warren and we never got the second half of breakfast, but lots of treats and yesterday's bones in the garden; I don't suppose it matters as I was rather full anyway. On Monday, we had a lovely walk and a long rest in spite of the thunder and lightning, no one seemed to mind, except Candy didn't like it, so I just went to the back of my cage and pretended it wasn't happening. I do like the security of my cage, particularly when it has the blue blanket over the top. Candy thought she had kennel cough, so I thought I might be getting it too, but today we are both much better and full of noise. I didn't bark at Tanya and Monty, but I did bark lots at Cyril and his bin, and there's a new yappy thing next door which set me off, so we all had to come inside and shut the door for a bit.

As it was Agility today, Candy went for the walk without me, and She took me on the lead along the lanes, to conserve my energy, She said. I got home very quickly, rather frustrated, so barked at everything including Richard, lots, but then he came in for coffee at the end, and She got cross when I barked at him indoors, so I went quiet until he got up to go and then I went wild. But not for long. I wasn't interested in Agility until She threw the ball and then I raced round like a mad thing and wouldn't come back, and when She did catch me, I wriggled out of my collar ~ now I know what I was conserving my energy for! But sometimes, I don't see the point of Agility and I don't like having to do what She wants and not what I want as I've done what I want all my life, more or less. We had a bit of a to-do when she tried to make me do something and physically moved me; I thought I'd bite her, but fortunately didn't, though I growled like anything. I Am Independent And Don't Like Doing What I don't Want To. She is perplexed as I am not interested in treats, toys or games, and just lie down and won't budge if She tries to make me do things. But I was very good when I was left in the car in the afternoon and I didn't try and get out or be silly at all. However, when she tried Training Exercises again, I just lay down. I'm winning!

In spite of a good start (I <u>just</u> wasn't sick in His car, but waited until I was in the car park at Sullington Warren; then I was sick twice) we had a horrid experience; a chocolate lab came up to us and made a grab for the, full, poo bag which She had in her hand, then dropped it when it realised what it was. The owner thought it was funny that all the poo fell onto the grass so She had to pick it up again, but She didn't think it funny at all; though She didn't say anything, I could sense it. A good walk after that, I was off-lead a lot of the time, and allowed myself to get caught in order to cross Water Lane main road, then off-lead again and met Her at the other side of the new bridge to have my lead put on to come home.

On Sunday, They had dinner in the dining room, all by themselves, no visitors, as Mark had suggested, so I was quite calm and didn't mind. I have bitten people in the dining room before as I don't like them there; there have been quite a lot of emails between Her and Mark about my behaviour and his suggestion was that I should get used to being in the dining room, on a regular basis without visitors there. I think the idea is so that I get used to the room first, and then add the people later, so I won't bite them again. And I didn't bark at the dishwasher either, so that's another hurdle overcome. But I still won't really do Training, though we had a game of sorts in the garden when She tried.

I've got a very upset tummy again, this time the other end. Wonder what it was? Kate came "to be barked at" in the afternoon; I have met her in the woods before which was all right, so I calmed down quite quickly, but I still bark when people leave.

On Tuesday, we had a lovely walk and I came back to have my lead put back on to come home; the only bad bit was when a Labrador puppy wanted to play chase and came to mouth my muzzle which I didn't like and then he started poking about at the other end which I definitely didn't like, but as I had the muzzle on I felt very unsafe so went to hide between Her legs. Chicken necks in the garden and then Tricia came round with a radio problem so I was put in my cage, but only barked a bit and she soon went away anyway.

Yesterday, I ran away from Daddy as it was his turn to take us out, and I wouldn't come back as I was having such fun chasing squirrels and barking like mad. He thought he'd lost me and rang Her, but I did turn up near the car park, and then ran away again so He couldn't catch me to put the lead back on. Did training in the afternoon, but indoors as I was barking at everything in the garden whilst She was gardening. I do get bored with training though. I think They were a bit fed up with me by the end. We've got the repaired television back, so are back in the sitting room for evenings, which is nice and things are getting normal again. Today was such a busy day; Richard came for gardening and coffee and I only barked at him a bit, and then the lawn man came and I hardly barked at him at all, even though he came very close to the conservatory windows. I do still let Them know that there are "people" about though. A bit more training and then Agility, where I did very well though it's quite hard work. I make Her work hard too, as I won't go over the jumps unless She goes with me, so we're both puffing at the end. I think I was good because of a mixture of just a short walk round the block on a lead, and liver cake rewards, plus a salmon biscuit from the teacher. Then we went on to Worthing where She went shopping, and I walked from the car park right through the town with all those people, scents and bikes and children on scooters, old ladies with wheelie trolleys and motorised wheelchairs. It was all rather much, and I did get very apprehensive, but we got back to the car all right and then came home. I slept for the rest of the day. And hadn't been sick!

We had a quick walk in Warren Hill today and then on to Barking Success for the day as They were going out for lunch a long way away. We were finally collected just before they closed; very glad to be home. I do like Barking Success and the people are lovely but I get a bit worried when other dogs go home and no one comes for us.

The next day, I was in the dog house again and it's not my fault, well, not all of it. I don't like Daddy's car which makes me feel sick, and She had forgotten this and gave us both a full breakfast, not the little tiny bit She usually does on a Saturday. I wasn't actually sick, but Daddy had to stop the car suddenly and we walked the rest of the way to Sullington Warren to be on the safe side. When we were well into the woods She let me off the lead and I had a lovely run and barked at "squirrels" but I wouldn't come back to be put on the lead and crossed Water Lane by myself. Fortunately, the van racing down the road avoided me, and the mini car coming the other way with a nice lady driver stopped to allow Her to catch me, but She wasn't pleased. I was very good after that. It was very hot by the time we got home so we all rested indoors in the shade, and then we had bones in the garden and I barked at everything that went up and down the track, even though I don't usually when I have a big bone to take my mind off Security. So, I was sent back indoors, and wouldn't give up my bone without a bit of a fuss, but Daddy was so fed up with my noise that he was having no nonsense, and I do know when I'm beaten. After tea, He went to watch the football scores and I went into the sitting room too, and tried to squeeze between the sofa and the coffee table, which I knocked over, spilling Daddy's tea and knocking Her lace pillow onto the floor. There are over 250 bobbins on that pillow, each with a fine silk thread, and some of them got muddled up and tangled, so, what with tea on the carpet (but fortunately not on the lace or I wouldn't be here to write this) the lace unworkable and the broken table leg, I think I'd better lie low for a bit. So, we had a very quiet night, no barking at all though there might have been foxes in the garden again, and that rabbit which I chase but never seem to catch. Then a very quiet morning even though Heather came for Pimms about lunch time and I was out of my cage and without a muzzle. Everyone was so pleased both with her for being so brave, and with me for being so restrained. I might have been forgiven for the coffee table. Late lunch in the dining room again, (Them) and ribs in the garden (us)!

I have a new strategy; as it was hot, humid and horrid, I came back on recall quite quickly on the walk as I didn't want to get exhausted. When She put me on the short lead at the Oak Tree, She took my muzzle off which was lovely and all the reward I needed. We all just sat around for the rest of the day.

My goodness doesn't seem to last long though; because today I seemed to lose Daddy in the woods, so he rang her and She came to look for me as he was too tired, and upset, to do so. We found each other quite quickly and when She'd put the lead on She took the muzzle off, again, for the short walk home, so that was nice. I'm not sure if I've been forgiven, but I think so. When it rained, we did a bit of Training; just Come, Sit, Round (to the Present position) and something with a paw which I don't understand.

As She was out most of today Daddy was in charge which wasn't a good idea because when the postman popped Her photos through the letter box, I started to chew the packaging, and when He saw me, I thought he was going to… well, I don't know what. Fortunately, I had only eaten the envelope and not the photos, so I live to see another day. Another case of "*Romanian câine nenorocit*" I fear, but He never says it even if he thinks it.

Thursday, 29th. It was a good day that just got better; I went for a lead walk while Candy went out into the woods with Daddy, and when we got back, She and I played a game of chase with my glucosamine tub ~ I ran down the hall with it and She had to chase me. Richard came to do the garden and I barked a bit but not that much, and then Candy came home and They had coffee. By now, the dog next door had been barking since 8.30 and I was getting tired of it, but I didn't bark back, and hardly barked at the post man because She told me not to. We did a bit of training and then there was Agility but it wasn't Agility but Flyball, which I've never done before. Before Agility, She had wanted to go to the loo in the garden centre where we park, so I had to go with Her, it's a good thing I'm a lady. But I didn't like the small cubicle space or the noisy taps and flushes and the hot air blower that made such a racket that I was glad when we left. I was quite animated in the Agility/Flyball ring and jumped all the row of jumps and carried the tennis ball back, so everyone was very pleased. Heather and Tricia with Bess and I were all in the ring together, though I was on a lead, but not with a muzzle so it was all friendly. I got so excited that I started to jump up and inadvertently caught Her hand with my teeth, but I didn't mean to hurt Her and She pretended it hadn't happened, except that there was blood everywhere. When we got home, They had tea in the garden and I got lots of treats because I didn't bark at anyone or anything and I get rewarded for keeping quiet. Talk about a day of experiences.

On Friday, we had a good long walk along the foot of The Downs where we met three horses, two going one way and one the other, so there was a collection of 3 horses, 4 dogs and 4 humans and I wasn't scared or bothered at all. I was off the lead quite a lot except for crossing Water Lane and on Badgers Holt where there are sometimes runners, but I came back to have my lead put on when necessary. Still not quickly though, and in my own good time. She gardened most of the afternoon, so we were in the garden too, with our big bones, so I didn't even bark at the yapping thing next door. Then today, we drove to Sullington Warren in Daddy's car, and I dribbled badly but wasn't sick as I had had such a small breakfast. We met a nice woman and her two rescue dogs and walked with them, and then they left to go home and we set off for our home until She tripped and fell flat down. She was hurt and very shaky but a nice man came and picked Her up and sorted her out, and I didn't mind, just sat and watched as I knew he was friendly. We came straight home and She did nothing for the rest of the day. She was surprised that I didn't mind a stranger coming over and helping her, but I would have minded if he hadn't been helping; She doesn't realise that I can tell what people are thinking.

In the garden. 24 August

****

11.08

Dear Dizzy,

Well I think "Congratulations" are in order on your 6-month survival! That's incredible how those 6/12 have flown by, and by the sounds of things there's not been a dull moment except perhaps when you pop into your cage/sanctuary for a bit of peace and quiet. There's a lovely photo of you in the cage looking very content and dare I say it – a tad pleased with yourself! So, thanks for sending that on. It also sounds as though you're gaining a huge amount of confidence which is great – well done you!

Mind you, you are extremely fortunate that *Her* and *Him* are able to give you so much time and all those lovely long walks and activities.

Sue xx

****

On 22 August, Dizzy wrote:

Dear frendvon

I am riting to u as a frend who has riten to me nicly becos I hav a problum.

I think She has lost it, *Sh*e has certunly lost my diary wot I rote with long words and proper punctushun, and it tuk owers to rite. She has lost chapters 17 and 18 and I fort u mite hav them to send bak to *Her* so I dont hav to bite her cos I'm cros

Candy is out so cant help me turn on the smellchek, but ive dun my best.

With luv and hugs,

Dizy

Reply on 23 August:
Willdomybest
A friend von

****

She says no one should be able to bend their spine as I can bend mine, in two directions at once!

Chapter Eight
September's Autumnal Events

Sunday, 1 September 2019. Daddy walks me on a Sunday and I wouldn't come back to him at the end of the walk, so he was a bit cross, and hurt. She did some training with me which was fun, but it's not the same as chasing squirrels. I think he is beginning to get tired of me, and my being naughty; he has always been at work or away when She has had new dogs in the past and doesn't realise what a lot of work it is; as I'm quite a lot collie I am very demanding and get bored easily so I make mischief. I can't help it, I really can't and I do try (Daddy says I'm very trying but I think that's a joke) but half the time I just can't see the point of what they want me to do, or why they want me to behave in such and such a way. And they don't speak Romanian, though their 'dog' is quite good. Candy says that she has told Her lots about where she came from before she was found as a stray in The New Forest, about the family with children, about the blue hatchback car that the family drove and about the walks along the various pebbly beaches in the Isle of Wight which is where she is supposed to have come from. She can also read various tail wags and ear positions, so there's hope for me yet even if she can't speak Romanian.

The next day, we met Heather and Bess on the way to the woods so walked with them, but then I seemed to get myself lost (I was too busy chasing squirrels to work out where I was) and only found Her as She was leaving the woods without me. I was a bit scared, but it won't stop me running off again! And Daddy was cross, again. The day after that was very odd; oh dear; a very curate's egg. Which reminds me, we sometimes get eggs for breakfast when She drops one on the floor; in fact, if we hear howls, it's usually because She's dropped something which we can gobble up. We set off for the seaside to meet Jane and Katie, and their new rescue dog from Greece called Rouli, but I was sick in the car just before we arrived. The sick smelled very much of sardines! After we were all cleaned up, Jane arrived and we set off for our walk along the sand as it was low tide. I had a lovely run with Katie, and also with Rouli, but I preferred Katie, and then some horses came cantering along and we all got very excited and I chased them and barked, but they were too far away so I came back and got put on the lead while the riders sorted themselves out and walked past. The older rider must have been the children's mother and she thanked us, a lot, but I'm not sure why. Then when the horses had passed and gone into the sea much further on, I was let off my lead and we all walked back along the greensward where horses aren't allowed; there were lots of dogs and children about, and even a cyclist, but I didn't bother with them and Katie and I just chased each other and had fun until she went catching mice. Katie catches a lot of mice and would eat them if she could. When we got back, They had coffee and herbal tea in the seaside café and we had water, and a bit of sausage from a man at the next table, and then as it was getting hot we came home, and I was sick again, just ten minutes from home. There wasn't anything in my tummy really so I don't know why I was sick. After lunch, She went to vacuum the car and I managed to squeeze out as the front door wasn't closed properly as the Henry-the-Hoover flex was in the way, and I went to say Hello to Monty who was walking back from his walk, and then when he got home I went exploring. Unfortunately, Caroline (Coco's Mum who lives nearby) found me in her garden and came to find Her, so I got caught and brought home. I am now exhausted, but not too tired to have made short work of my tea-time ribs in the garden.

On Wednesday, it was so wet I couldn't even be bothered to get out of bed, and I certainly didn't want to go for a walk, but it got better as it eventually stopped raining and the sun came out. Carole came round for coffee after our walk; I have met her once or twice in the woods, but not much since her dog died, but I was so good and only barked for a few seconds. I didn't even bark when she got up to look at the garden, nor when she left, and I didn't bother to check the premises to make sure she had actually gone. I did bark at the postman though! Heather popped round to give Them information about looking after their tortoise while they are away, and I was out of my cage and without a muzzle because Heather's nice and not a threat at all. In the evening, they went out, and came back with some people I didn't know, so I was back in my cage; he was nice and calm, but she was a bit apprehensive so I got very cross and barked fiercely at her, which made her worse, which made me worse too. She kept getting up to go out to the loo, which didn't help; but I did calm down eventually.

No Agility yesterday because when we got into the car, I immediately felt sick and dribbled and yawned and fussed, so we turned round and came home, so no walk and no Agility; not a good day, though we did play ball in the garden for a bit and then Lyn came so I barked at her instead. Today, we walked round the Downs and then went to Barking Success as the men had arrived to treat the lawn and I didn't like them. They had gone by the time we were collected after lunch and we all then had to stay indoors because of the stuff the lawn men had used, but it didn't matter as it was raining. Daddy went out so She made lace and we went to sleep. She took me to my first training classes in the village hall in the evening, but there was no one there as it had been cancelled, so we came home and had a sort of game with my tuggy. I won't tug it with Her but will play with it on my own, and kill it. These are, or will be, new classes with new people, and neither of us knows what to expect. Candy was left at home as she is supposed to know it all anyway. Then strangely, we did our evening wees down the lane on our leads, and not in the garden at all which seemed to be covered in soil and smelly things.

We had to do our wees down the lane the next day as well, something seems to have gone on in the garden and we're not allowed onto it. I wonder about our bones. And I seem to have been started on my CBD oil drops again, twice a day, which I don't like but it might make me better in the car. I came when called on our walk and for the final leg I didn't have my muzzle on which was nice when the Old Man gave me a biscuit; I could eat it easily. Bones indoors again and lead walks from the front door all the time. What is going on? There was a lot of walking along our verges in the evening too; I don't know what for; Candy weed but I didn't so we were shut in the kitchen/conservatory/utility room for the night with newspaper down in the utility room, just in case of accidents. What accidents? I "was dry all night" but did do a wee on the verge this morning to enormous praise from everyone. Walked with Daddy this morning and had a few Quavers when he had his Sunday G&T, a nice treat for both of us. Still can't go in the garden even though it was a lovely sunny day. She gardened, but out in the lane not inside the fence.

By Monday, I had finally got the message and weed on the grass verge in the front because we still aren't allowed on any of the lawns. Walk in the woods in the pouring rain, and in through the front door again to avoid walking on the grass even though we had wet paws on the hall carpet. Indoors and bored and rain, rain, rain. Knocked over the coffee table again, and this time really broke its leg properly, and tied Her lace in even more knots than before. I think I know why I'm called Disaster. She won't get cross even though it takes ages and ages to untie all the lace muddle, but Daddy gets very cross on her behalf and I really am beginning to have problems with him. I wouldn't wee on the verge this evening as I didn't want to, so we got shut in the kitchen again for the night. I played with a tennis ball by myself in the sitting room this evening for the first time.

As I had refused to come back on the walk with Daddy and wouldn't listen to him, it made him cross and grumpy. I got almost all the way home too, without a lead, though I did chase a car to the car park. I had begun to chase a runner in the woods, but did come back in the end, and didn't bite him, but Daddy was a bit rattled. Runner was cross too, and the language went blue!!! Romanian again, "*Pleacă de aici, câine nenorocit*"; whilst I miss Romania, I don't miss the bad language and nastiness. We are still having bones and things indoors and having to go out on leads to wee in the lane. I wonder how long this will last?

Things are better today though; we went in the car to Sullington Warren and had a lovely off-lead walk home. And a lovely chase game with another dog and came back to have the lead put on to cross the road, then off again in Sandgate Park until the road; but I went into the pond first and splashed two children when I shook. They screamed and giggled. It is so good to find people who seem to like me and have fun with me; so different from the past.

Sunday is Daddy's walking day and he was cross as I ran away from him again and wouldn't come back for ages; I also chased a runner who was in the woods, so I think I'm in disgrace. They went out for a very long lunch, but while they were loading the car with food to take, I slipped out and met next door's dogs who were going for a walk, and set off for a bit with them, but soon lost interest and came home. The foxes were so noisy all night I hardly slept, and therefore neither did anyone else. And the next morning, I ran away, again; we met Rebecca and Alfie in the lane and walked to the woods with them, and when Alfie and Candy were let off their leads, so was I, and I just took off. They went and spoiled things by going a different way, but I still chased squirrels and barked at things, and then I couldn't find them, so came home. Very cross and upset all day, and barked at everything. By Tuesday, I did proper Recall training on the walk, and other bits on the long, long lead. And was patted by three very tiny children. So I can be good, sometimes. When it suits me!

I got to Agility without being sick, though I did a lot of yawning and a bit of dribbling in the car; it was a bit better on the homeward journey. Agility has become Flyball which I like better, and I can really get up speed going in one direction, though I am more nervous coming the other way, don't even ask why. She thinks it's because the wire netting is closer to the end of the run one way than it is the other, and She wonders whether I'm afraid I might run into the wire; silly really as it's really a long way away. I came when called in the ring, too, and enjoyed the afternoon. We are still not allowed into the garden which is getting very tiresome, I can hear and scent the foxes but as I'm on the lead and stuck indoors I can't get at them!

Friday, 20 September 2019. A lovely walk, on and off the lead in Sandgate Park; I started to chase a runner while She was busy pulling up Himalayan Balsam and wasn't concentrating, but the runner stopped which allowed Her to grab me until she had run on and out of sight. No worries there, as the runner also had her own dog which chased her. When we got to the lake at the exit from the Park, I came so She could put the lead back on, the short lead, so I could have my muzzle off and we walked nicely back home. Just opposite our house, a nice man was doing something in the garden and called us over for treats, we sat and got lots of cuddles and biscuits, and then he asked why I was being so good as I had such a dreadful reputation, and She explained that it was because he had no fear or tension, was calm, and wasn't in our house or driveway, and after a bit he asked if he could kiss me!!! She said that that would be pushing his luck, but he did it anyway, so I bit him. He loomed over me and I was scared. She should have said NO in a very firm voice to him when he asked, instead of being polite, and he did admit that the fault was his, but it made Her upset, and so are we all now. Apparently, he had to go to hospital and have 16 stitches, and a tetanus injection; the stitches are in his beard so don't show up. He says he won't report me, which is very kind and good of him, because I might be taken away if he does.

I was afraid that after yesterday, I might not be allowed out again, but we went, as usual, to Sullington Warren where I had a lovely run off-lead, and then came back to cross Water Lane into Sandgate Park where I was off-lead again. And came back again. Met the rescue dog from Nigeria again (who is called DB), with the other one and their mum; They had a long chat and so I approached the mum as she wanted me to, but DB wasn't best pleased and tried to bite me. I jumped back so all was well, but I was happy to go back on the lead after that as I get some confidence from it. Tricia came round to collect her paper and after an initial bark I went quiet.

Hooray, I have learned how to get my muzzle off! It took a lot of wiggling and rubbing it on the ground, which made it very dirty but I didn't mind. She has also taken the blue cover-all-blanket off my cage so I can now see out, and try not to bark.

I forgot to say that a week or so ago, I learned how to wag my tail when anyone is talking to me, which makes people happy. And it's a proper wag from side to side, in fact, when I do it really properly it almost hits me in the face. At the end of my walk today, I wasn't happy at all because, although it had been a lovely calm and quiet walk, we met a truck, not a very big one and it was going very slowly, but I got very scared and tried to kill it. Not a good idea; I was out with Daddy and he had me on a very short lead so no one came to any harm, but I was unsettled all day and snarled at Tracey as she walked home from work, and I've met her lots of times before.

Agility was cancelled again today because the wind kept blowing all the jumps over, so we went for an extra walk in the woods, which was nice. I came back to Her a few times and then had my lead put back on and my muzzle off which was also nice. Rhia came for a bit in the evening and after some barking I relaxed and snored! When she had gone, and I didn't bark at all, She and I played Mad Maude, chasing a tuggy up and down the hallway, She threw it and I chased and killed it, and then just as it was getting too, too exciting, we had ribs in the utility room to calm down.

Friday, 27th. My goodness, what a day! First, we walked round Sandgate Park in the pouring rain and got very wet, but I stopped at the lake to have my lead put back on, and my muzzle off, and then barked at the ducks. But I'd been quiet all morning so it was all right; then we met Rebecca and walked home with Alfie, then met Odin, and finally Bess who was looking out of the window, so I jumped up outside and she jumped up inside and it was a lot of fun. Then in the afternoon, between showers we went out in the car to a field, but I'm not sure why. I think we were supposed to do Recall training, but as my harness was sopping wet from this morning She had left it over a radiator to dry and the training woman wouldn't do Recall just on a collar, so it was all a bit of a waste of time, except we did Touch and I got lots of treats. When we got back home, and I wasn't sick in the car because She had used an Adaptil spray, there was a phone call, so after a cup of tea we rushed off again to the village hall for "school" in the hall. This was my first time at "school" and what was nice was that there was only one other dog there so I didn't feel crowded. I did heel-on-lead, lead Recall, Sit and Down and Wait. It was all right walking anticlockwise as there was wall, Her, me and lots of space which I liked, but when we went clockwise, I was next to the wall and got all scared because I had nowhere to escape to, so I stopped and refused to go any further. She put me in the middle of the room in a lie-down until I was composed again. It was all very new, but quite fun and I walked really quickly on lead which was good. I think she walked fast so I had to keep up and couldn't find the time to get difficult. It's easier to concentrate in the Hall than at home where there are so many more distractions.

The next day when Daddy dropped us at Sullington Warren for our walk home and drove off, I didn't want to go into the woods and wanted to follow him so that we were all together. There was a bit of a muddle at the gate because a man called to Her and told Her not to bother latching it as he was coming through, which he did, and then stopped to pat me, but I didn't like it as there was nowhere to run to so I lunged at him to make him go away. There was no damage done as I was still on the lead, and had my muzzle on, but he and She were a bit rattled and I stayed on my lead until we got to the big bowl of grass in the middle and the man had gone so I was let off the lead, but kept quite close to Her all the way back to the road when I waited to have my lead put back on. Then we crossed Water Lane and went into Sandgate Park when I was off-lead again but still stayed quite close and didn't bark at a woman with a baby in a pram, and asked to be put back on the lead long before we got to the lake. We had bones in the back garden again as we used to do in the past, so perhaps we're allowed there now.

They discovered last night that I'd weed twice on the dining room carpet, again, so the atmosphere was a bit strained. Then I tried to attack the television when the ITV logo came on, I don't like ITV. Today wasn't much better, a very polite runner came up behind us on the walk and called out that he was there, She foolishly asked him to walk past me, but I still tried to bite him even though I had a muzzle on, but was off the lead. She put me straight back on for about ten minutes until She was sure he'd gone and the we continued the walk and I barked at everything; I was very wired today. I came back to have my lead put back on, and we walked home without any problems, but I can see she is worried about the muzzle/lead business ~ and I certainly don't want to spend the rest of my walking life on lead and with a muzzle so we don't know how to resolve it. I just can't relax properly.

****

27 September

Hi Ann,

I just wanted to say, when we past in the lanes, I thought wow, great progress on Dizzy. Well done you!

Have a great day,

Stefanie

****

27 September

Good evening

It was a pleasure to meet you and Dizzy today, I am totally in love with her!! I wanted to share the photos I took of her as they are just lovely!

See you soon!

Lucy (dog trainer)

****

Chapter Nine
October Days

Tuesday, 1 October 2019. A bit of a mixed sort of day; a lovely walk and I was so good when we met a couple of horses, but on the way up Hampers Lane the bin lorry was behind us and didn't give us time to find a driveway to hide in; he was right behind us and very aggressive, then the binman got out to collect the bin and I completely lost it barking and lunging, and generally carrying on. I was so scared and rattled that I barked at every car and person that came past after that. We went to see Kate in her house down the road and I played in her garden and sniffed all round, and barked at imaginary squirrels next door, then we went in for coffee and I tried to fight one of the nest of tables when it was moved, but because I had my muzzle on I couldn't get at it. Then I settled down on Penny's old dog cushion and went to sleep. I had made friends with Kate before, in the garden, and They were just talking so I got bored, but the phone rang so I went to answer it as no one else was going to, but it stopped so I came back into the sitting room. When we got up to go, I got very cross and barked at the two horses that I could see through the window, just at the bottom of the garden in the field, and I didn't like that at all, but I did calm down and we went outside to get into the car. Only I didn't want to get into the car so I raced off into the woods to chase things, and there were rabbits there too, and I wouldn't come back, even though They were calling me. Eventually, I did come back to the back gate into the garden and barked for Kate to let me in; she put my lead on and as we walked back to the car I turned on her and tried to bite her as I felt squashed in the confined space between the house wall and the car, and she had a stick to help her walk. I came home feeling very sorry, and had a quiet afternoon and evening. I think Kate was sorry too, but for a different reason.

Today, I frightened myself by getting stuck under the middle-size of the nest of three tables here at home which is doing service as a coffee table while the proper one is away being mended. Then, as Daddy's feet were the nearest thing to me I thought I might bite them in retaliation, but thought better of it. When Kate came to the front door with the photos she had promised to show Her, I went quite mad and barked furiously, which included taking a bite out of the sitting room door, again; we had been in the sitting room when she arrived and I was shut in there with Daddy as security. He was not best pleased. Rhia arrived in the evening which was nice; after a bit of carrying on, I just turned my back on them all and settled down in my cage. Rhia is very calming.

We called in to deliver something to Jo who I hadn't met before; she's nice and gave me lots of fussing, and I liked it and didn't mind at all, though I was a bit wary of her husband. They have squirrels in their garden! I did lunge at a lone man on the way home; he had no dog, no camera and was striding determinedly along which I didn't like. Agility/Flyball was really fun and I'm getting really good at it; we did the Flyball jumps in one direction and the Agility jumps coming back in the other. I am still on lead for much of the time, but as the lead keeps knocking the jumps over, we did some lead-free as well. Tricia asked Jay if we could swap dogs so that she would work me and She could work Bess, but She said NO as I didn't have my muzzle on and She thought I wasn't ready yet. She was right.

Today was not a good day really; we met Bess on the way up the road and walked together to Sandgate Park, but I lunged at runners (two), cyclist (one), man with dog in a push chair (I kid you not), and almost every car for which I lost count. But I was lovely when we met Brenda as she gives me treats, and I allowed her to fuss me, too. Big bones in the garden in the rain, and then the TV man came; I was shut in my cage but only barked a bit. He did go in and out of the house quite a lot, but was very quiet, so I ignored him after a minute or two. I did need to check that he had quite gone though, when he did leave. Dog school in the evening and I think I did quite well, though R (the teacher) thought I was given too many treats!

I think the Adaptil must work as I was sick in the car again today going to Sullington Warren for the start of our walk, and as it's only a couple of miles She hadn't bothered to use the spray. We met the other Romanian street dog, called Millie, on our walk, She and her mum are lovely. Apparently, Millie, who has lived here for six years, still can't let guests go home without trying to bite them as they leave, but her owner knows that now and takes action. Nice walk until we met the post van and I tried to eat his tyres. When we got home, Heather came to collect the paper and I was out of my cage and had no muzzle; there were no problems and I even let her out of the house without getting stressed. As we hadn't had breakfast in case I was sick in the car, I was expecting to have breakfast when we got home, but She forgot all about it until mid-afternoon, so We Are Starving! Then She left the front door open by mistake (it had swollen in the damp and doesn't shut properly unless you slam it) and I chased away up the track to the house at the top where the woman there screamed obscenities at us; Candy was there as well as she had followed us. I started to chase their cat but it jumped over the fence and got away. I got scared by the shouting and went back to Her though I had had no intention of doing so at first.

Sunday didn't seem to be a holiday day at all; games in the hall first, then leadwork on the driveway and gardening, with bones. I dug lots of holes in the flower bed, sending plants and bulbs flying all round; She wasn't happy. Again!

Monday, 7th. I've been here eight months today. I celebrated by refusing to come back as I was busy chasing squirrels on our walk. Someone on the walk asked if I was improving and She said I was making great strides … but backwards! Did some training on the drive when it wasn't raining. After tea, She left the front door a bit open, again, so I got out, again, and dashed back up the track, again, and got screamed at, again. I think this is so much fun and the woman gets so very cross and agitated, but She never answers back so the woman gave up in the end. The woman was slightly confused because she was actually cross with Candy who had come up the track to see what was going on and was just sitting there. I wonder how many times I can get away with this game? It's such fun and Candy gets the blame!

She took us out as Daddy was poorly today and we went along the Downs so I was on my lead all the time, but very freaked out all day. I barked at lorries and cars, and when we got home, I barked at everything else! We had met Rebecca with Alfie in the woods and she had said that all the dogs in the woods were misbehaving, so I think it must have been the imminent thunder, which we never got, but it was oppressive and tense. Also, I was worried about Daddy being unwell. I did lead training on the driveway again.

It was Her yoga class today, so Daddy had had to get better in order to take us on our walk, but I didn't want to go so we only got to the end of the lane and I sat down and wouldn't budge. He managed to get me moving but I stopped again before the car park, and again at Anxiety Corner, so he brought us home, and when he had gone out of the room, I jumped onto the conservatory sofa to see out of the window so I could see and bark better. Driveway training again. And a cross Daddy!

A day or two later, I did some long-line-recall-training, and was very, very good to the whistle, but as soon as She let me off the lead, I ran away and chased squirrels because for the two previous days I'd been on a lead. But I did come back at the end of the walk when we met Heather with Bess and I had my lead put on as good as gold. Heather came round to collect some mushrooms She had bought and I let her into the house and got petted and then let her out again with no barking at all. Made up for it though in the garden later when I barked at everything.

Today, we had a dripping wet walk, lots off-lead and I needed the run. Not many squirrels about, but I did find one to bark at. Friday School in the evening and I was very good, even though there was a very barking one-year-old cocker who upset me. I hope we progress to something a bit more interesting than heel-on-lead; in the end, I got bored and lay down, refusing to move; then I rolled onto my back with my feet in the air and still wouldn't budge. She just laughed at me though, and so did everyone else, so I think I got away with it.

Saturday, 12th. What a peculiar day; early morning walk with no breakfast beforehand, then sitting around whilst They had coffee and talked on the phone, then into Daddy's car and off for miles and miles. I sat in the front on Her lap but was still sick just a few miles before we arrived, after a good hour and a half in the car. She had sprayed Adaptil in good time, and I had had lots of pills in cheese, but it just didn't quite work. We arrived at a car park with grassy bits and waited, walking round and round this area until another car arrived; I remembered Andrew, and had nipped Tracey, but had never met Murphy who is a German Pincher, very rare and awfully posh. We ignored each other in the car park, got back into the cars and went to a restaurant for lunch, where we were all very good. So was the food. Then we got back into the cars for a minute's journey to houses by the sea where They all went inside to look around, for ages and ages, while Murphy, Candy and I stayed in our cars, then we all went for a run on the beach as the tide had gone out and there was lots of sandy shingle. I had to have my muzzle on, but was off-lead; Murphy wanted to play chase but I was a bit nervous as he is . bigger than I am, and didn't have a muzzle whilst I did. There were children on the beach in spite of the rain, but I didn't bother with them at all. Then we got back into the cars, again, and went for a few minutes to another cafe place where we went inside, again, to dry off and They had tea and I had more pills as I'd sicked up the others. We were all very good again, and finally, we got back into our cars to come home, and I managed not to be sick until a mile, or just a bit less, from home. And I still haven't had breakfast, or any food except my bed-time biscuits. I was exhausted and almost immediately after arriving home I rolled into a ball, collapsed into a heap and went to sleep for a couple of hours in the hall, later though they did all go into the sitting room to warm up after She lit the stove, but I was too tired to move until about 10 pm. Let's hope tomorrow is calmer.

After yesterday, I couldn't wake up; I missed my morning pee and biscuit and refused to go on a walk. Anywhere. It was after lunch that Daddy got me into the garden to wee, then I came straight back in and back to sleep. Suddenly, it's night time and bed time. Good!

Today is back to normal; wet walk in the rain. When we were supposed to be coming home at the end, I ran off, but started coming back via lots of gardens, then into Caroline's garden at the end of our lane and then up our lane to the neighbour's who doesn't like me but I did come back with no harm done, I hope. Bones. Bored in spite of a bit of training in the sitting room. And it's still raining.

At last it is dry so our walk out in Sandgate Park was better, where, unlike the Woods, I do come back at the end of the walk to have my lead put on. I've got used to running away in the Woods, and once a habit is set, it's hard for me to change. A very unsettling late afternoon/evening because it had started to rain again so, as there were no decent programmes on the television, She put a disk in the CD player and played a tape of all of Tara's litter, right from when they were born to about ten weeks old. Tara (Hero's Star) was a dog some years before me and one of her puppies was called Mayhem who I "replaced". Actually, I don't think I replaced her very well as she was a competition dog and not bad at it. I barked and barked at the television as the puppies were squeaking and I didn't understand what was going on; I was very scared and hid under the coffee table. When they went to get supper, and had long since turned the television off, I went behind it and barked all evening as I didn't know where the puppies had gone. I was Very Upset.

Today, They came back from lunch with friends, and brought the friends in; I did bark as I've only seen them once, I think, before, but I soon settled down and they said how much better I was than last time. I was still in my cage, but it's not really a problem. Did a bit of Weaving-round-legs in the evening when everyone had gone back home.

It is a Thursday so I barked madly at Richard who comes on Thursdays to help in the garden; he had arrived early and was already in the driveway. I have to go into my cage when he's here, as I try (and sometimes succeed) in biting him, but had been on a road walk with no muzzle before he arrived, and was so good, I didn't bark at cars or people, and only a tiny *wuff* at a young boy on a bike. Then we had another man in the garden as well, so I really barked then, and then after lunch Lyn came, so it's been a very noisy day. Did weaving. Getting the hang of it though I still don't see the point, but it keeps Her happy.

We met Gill and the Gang today, not having seen them for ages. Because Gill is a dog person, she doesn't make me anxious so I was very good and came back when called; there aren't many people around who really understand dogs, but she's one of them who does. So, I don't panic and really behave well. Usually.

On a lovely day, I ran around Sandgate Park for almost an hour without a lead and had a lovely time, meeting Her at the exit gate to have my lead put on and my muzzle taken off. As She was picking up her gloves and my muzzle, a runner came up behind us to the gate that we were in front of, so I panicked as she was so close, and ran back and nipped her, and then knew I shouldn't have and wished I hadn't. The runner wasn't really cross, but was a bit upset. When we met Madeleine a bit later on, I was as good as can be and let her make a fuss of me though She watched me like a hawk all the time. Dawn came for coffee, we've met in the lane a few times but she's never been here since I came, and although I barked at her for a bit, I soon stopped and turned my back on them all; I even didn't bark when Dawn left to go home, and didn't need to check the house to make sure she had actually gone. Went to Andy-the-lovely-vet to discuss my motion sickness and various remedies, and I heard Her ask him whether I ought to be put to sleep as I was so unreliable. He just said, "No, just leave a muzzle on her all the time," and when She queried whether I'd mind, he said no, I wouldn't. I wish someone would ask me directly! School in the evening and I was good again and did a wonderful Recall, twice, once when She was looking the other way. Lots of people make a fuss of me there too, and said how good I was, and I Don't Wear A Muzzle At Training!

Saturday, 19 2019. It was a bit of a thoughtful night really; I had hoped to book the vet's appointment for Monday to discuss the motion vs anxiety sickness in the car, but Friday was the first space they had with the vet I wanted. By then, she had had bitten the runner. I didn't/don't really want her to have to spend the rest of her life outside with a muzzle on, but it just looks as if there is no alternative as the crises develop so quickly ~ it must have been a split second between taking the muzzle off and arranging the lead (which was attached to her) in the correct hand, which is when the runner crashed into view. I was surprised that the runner didn't see me, standing in front of, and definitely in the way of the gate, but I can't go on making excuses for her as I have been doing so far. Every time there's been an "incident", however minor, there has been a reason for her behaviour, but I really can't expect the whole world to revolve around what upsets what is, after all, only a dog. But when I mentioned this to the vet with the phrase "I'm exhausted and anxious and depressed, and just can't keep doing this", he was very authoritative; I do believe the vets' lives would be easier if there were only animals and no owners at all in their surgeries! We didn't even discuss strategies, he just told me to get on with things. The silly thing was that she was so good in class in the evening, putting up with lots of feet, and doing perfect Recalls. But then at night, while I was in the office finishing off stuff on the computer, and Tony was in the bedroom, there was the most awful fight outside the kitchen door; I suspect Candy had invaded what Dizzy thought of as "her" space, but whilst Candy was a fighter in her youth, she's an old lady now and was really upset. Tony and I were furious, and Candy took refuge in our bedroom with Dizzy relegated to the hallway and bless her, she didn't even try and push her luck to come in. She is very subdued this morning.

It's Sunday again so I had a fun walk with Daddy, but he didn't; as he keeps me on the lead because I won't come back when he calls, I decided I wasn't walking with him, so as soon as we were in the woods, I did my usual trick and sat firmly down. He pulled my lead; I was behind him, so managed to wriggle out of my harness and was free. Yippee! Then, later, he tried to catch me as I was barking at squirrels with my front paws up the tree, and when he had got almost to hold me, I glared at him and he backed off, I think he was scared of me. I've not noticed that before. Heather and Tricia came for lunch, I hardly barked at all, but was in my cage to start off with, and then when they all went into the dining room, I came out but with my muzzle on. Not necessary at all, I thought, but I think they were happier that way. Watched rugby all evening.

After a quiet weekend, we had a very short walk today in the woods where we met Gill and The Gang, but it ended badly as I wouldn't come back and, off-lead, began to run home getting in the way of Gill's car in the car park, whose wheels I tried to bite as she was driving her dogs home. Back home, I dug up the bone that Candy had buried in the garden, and she came for it and we had a real, real fight with teeth and I was not letting go. In the end, She came and hit me with the lead, She's never hit me before so I was shocked and let go, and surprised. In the afternoon, we all went for a walk with Jane, Katy and Rouli at Cissbury Ring, and we got there without my being sick, though we did travel at a stately 30 mph, and were even overtaken by a trailer with a tractor on it. I wasn't sick on the way home either, though I did dribble a lot. A few days later at the beach, we had a lovely run with Katy and Rouli for about 90 minutes before it began to drizzle, and I came back to have my lead put on when She called me, and then we came home. I can be really good when I decide to be, but that's not very often.

Oh dear, life seems to be going backwards again, because of yesterday and Gill, She won't let me off the lead in the woods either now. So now I have my muzzle on all the time and am on a long lead in the woods all the time too, though I can still run about elsewhere, because I come back to have the usual lead put on at the end of the walk. Walked in Sullington Warren today though, so that was all right as I behave better there. However, the next day it was Daddy's turn, and we got as far as the Warren Hill car park and I sat down, so he just gave in and let me off the lead and I was really good, I chased squirrels but came back to have my lead put back on at the end of the walk. Daddy was impressed, and we got on a lot better. He took me out on Thursday too and I did the "won't budge" trick again. I know that if he tries to pull me along towards him, I can wriggle out of my harness, so he has to let me off or we'd be there still! But I do come back at the end, so he doesn't mind too much. Then we went to kennels, again, but I don't mind as I like it there, and they like us.

****

19 October

Hello Tony and Ann,

Glad to hear you are managing to battle the wet weather!

It sounds a more positive report for her this week and I'm wondering if those antisickness pills are the way to go if it makes her so sleepy!

Poor little monkey; I don't know how you do it.

133

So cute!!!

Chapter Ten

November Remember,
Remember the 5th of November!

Saturday, 2 November 2019. As soon as the kennels opened, They came to get us! It was a very strange day as we all camped in the sitting room round the stove as the boiler had broken down while they'd been away so there was no heat or hot water, and the storms blew the television aerial down and it banged against the window which frightened me a lot so I barked at it, but that didn't seem to stop it banging, so I stopped barking, but didn't like it a bit. When the storm was less, we had breakfast (about 3 pm) and went into the woods for a run, and then dashed back home to the fire again! I still won't come back at the end of the walk and She says "something will have to be done". I wonder what?

Today was lovely and sunny after yesterday, what storms? Daddy took us out and I did my usual trick of refusing to move, but we had met Heather on the way to the woods, so between them, and Bess, I was persuaded to walk on lead as far as the car park, and when it was safe, I was let off. I kept everyone in sight all day as I didn't want them to disappear again; even when we got back home, I sat on Her feet so She wouldn't go anywhere. There were fireworks in the evening which I barked at, but not out of fear as much as surprise! They went on for ages and ages, but we all settled down when they were over. Even Candy seemed better about them than usual and didn't try to hide.

I don't know what got into me today; we went to Sandgate Park, where I always come back to have my lead put on at the end of the walk, but today I was chasing squirrels (there weren't any as it was raining) so wouldn't come back no matter how long She waited and called. Then a gamekeeper-man came past and made a funny little squeaky whistle, and I came to find out what the noise was so she put me on the lead straight away. He said it sounded like a rabbit in distress and attracts dogs every time. When we got home, another man came to mend the aerial and I barked at him and tried to attack him through the conservatory window by standing on the sofa when he went past in the garden with a ladder, She was furious, but I did it again when he passed the conservatory window a second time. Eventually, he went and things returned to sort of normal in that although the house is cold, at least the television works!

We met Heather and Bess at the end of the drive today so walked in the woods with them. Candy barked and barked but I was quite good, I was also kept on the lead as we were having a short walk as Fiona was coming for coffee and She didn't want me running off. I hadn't met Fiona before, but she's the sort of person I like, calm and unfussed, so I only barked a bit and then settled down with, eventually, my back to them all. I didn't even bark when she got up to leave; They were so pleased. We went for a second walk this afternoon after our ribs in the garden; as the walk was a bit short this morning, I didn't have my harness on, so we all just kept walking, to the car park, where we were both let off our leads. I ran off as usual, and didn't come back for ages and ages, and was so puffed when I caught up with them that I was happy to go back on the lead for a few minutes, then She let me off again (in the belief that if she did this enough, I might realise that the lead wasn't the end of the walk, fat chance of that.) I was off like a shot, barked madly at squirrels who were everywhere, and wouldn't come back at all. She got cross in the end and said She was going home anyway, so I ran to catch up. I should have gone on the lead there and then, but managed to escape having got side-tracked by another squirrel in a garden in Sanctuary Lane and She wasn't going to chase me round someone else's garden so carried on home. I don't mind being left behind as I know my way home, and was walking up the drive as She came back out to find me, having left Candy back at home. It got very noisy with fireworks at night and Candy was really scared and tried to hide in cupboards and behind things, but I didn't really mind at all as I knew I was safe at home and no harm would come to me here.

For some reason, today we played "ball-in-the-hall" before breakfast, I love chasing it and although I pick it up, I don't bother to bring it right back so She has to come and collect it from me. Andy the plumber came to fix the boiler; he was here for ages and I barked most of the time even though She and I and Candy were in the sitting room out of the way, and I bit chunks out of the door trying to get at him. He is terrified of me. I calmed down a bit when Daddy came to take over because he makes more of a fuss of me than She does, stroking me and calming me down. Exhausted by the evening.

As it is Thursday today, we had a short walk because of Agility in the afternoon. Richard didn't come because he thought it was going to rain, but realised, too late, that perhaps he should have done, so came and knocked on the door anyway. That was a big mistake because a doorbell ring starts us both off and then I get hysterical. She chased me up and down the hall trying to get me into the kitchen so I'd be out of the way before She opened the door, but I didn't want to go so it was a bit of a tussle, and I barked like mad. No wonder Richard is scared. She won in the end though. Agility was actually Flyball and I'm getting really good and enjoying it but I still can't see the point of bringing the ball back over all the jumps, so either drop it or run out. Although I wasn't sick going to Findon, I dribbled and fidgeted coming back; all the treats perhaps?

Today, we had a walk in Sandgate Park, and I was outsmarted! I went off-lead as usual, and to begin with we went the usual way, but then She changed direction and we left the Park through the gate onto Sandgate Lane, and it was all fenced round so I couldn't escape and She caught me to put the lead back on. We came back through the tile works and along the lanes which we haven't done for ages and then, in Bracken Lane it began to all go wrong; a woman with straggly grey hair came up behind us in her car and wouldn't give us time to get into a driveway, and then roared past. I tried to bite her tyres, as I do, and she shouted something rude out of her window. It took to the T junction at the end of the lane to settle us down as Candy was barking her head off as well, and so we waited at the side of the road for the traffic jam that this woman was causing at the junction of Bracken and Hampers Lanes ~ there were cars and vans and all sorts turning in all directions, and I got so scared I just went crazy, and so did Candy. All the cars came too close and lots of the drivers were cross, so the tension was palpable, and then a van driver was lost and wanted directions but She wouldn't talk to him as I was trying to kill him and the car. Then a big Jeepy thing came and stopped by us and the man talked to Her and I got upset all over again. When we got home, I went into my cage to calm down, and a few minutes later, the Jeep man came in for coffee. I went crazy, but finally calmed down as They all seemed to be getting on, until he went to get his electrician's bag when I barked again, but he began work in the sitting room so I calmed down as I was in my cage in the conservatory. After he had gone, we had ribs in the garden, and in the evening as it was a Friday I went to classes, where I was bored so got naughty and ran off, or just lay down on my back with my feet in the air and everyone laughed. So R decided we should do "send-aways" (otherwise known as "go to bed in your basket") which I got a bit scared of and confused about. I was supposed to run, away, towards a box area made by chairs, to a treat on the floor, but the treat was too near the back wall and I wasn't going into a trap. It was a bit better when She moved the treat forward. It seems silly; She has spent months getting me to come to Her and now She wants me to go Away. People? I was sick in the car coming home, too, all the way from the Village Hall, just about a mile.

Editor's Note: Goodness knows what's happened to her in the past, but she definitely doesn't like to feel boxed-in; this emphasises her unwillingness to run the Flyball jumps one way. She will dash down them towards the open end of the training area, but is very hesitant about coming back towards the fence, even though she is supposed to be concentrating on holding the ball and the fence is still some distance away.

I barked for two hours during the night, but stopped as soon as She came into the conservatory to see what all the noise was about; now we're all tired! I think today, She's quite lost it; first She put on my new collar, and then five minutes later took it off again. Then She did it again, and again. I've no idea what's going on.

This is the next day and the same ritual with the collar ~ hey ho! Their grandson William came for lunch and although I barked at first, I stopped as he is very calming and fed me sprats, and then when they all sat down to eat, I went to sleep. He left at tea time and I was allowed out of my cage, and we had ribs in the garden. We all watched television in the evening and I thought I might bite Her when her foot touched me, but didn't. I had been having a dream earlier, when, She said, I was wagging my tail even though I was asleep. That's a first.

On Tuesday, I had a lead walk with lots of Recalls and then some people called Juliette and Tim and Di came for coffee; I hadn't really met any of them before so barked quite a lot but settled down eventually. Di hasn't had dogs so was a bit apprehensive of all the noise but they all chatted and laughed so I relaxed until it was time for them to go. Unfortunately, Tim came to my side of the coffee table on his way out so I went crazy and although he did notice, he didn't make a fuss which was good of him. It rained and blew all day so we had quick ribs but were mostly indoors.

Because it was Wednesday, Candy and I went to Barking success while She went to yoga and Daddy came to collect us. Nice day but glad to be home.

For some reason, today is a special day so we walked to Washington; it was pouring with rain and we all got very wet and when we got there, we dripped all over the village hall floor but they didn't seem to mind though they wouldn't let us vote, only Her. A difficult walk home getting drowned by a car crashing through a puddle in the road next to us, so we were all a bit cross. We met eleven cars in Sanctuary Lane, which is designated a bridleway, and had to get out of the way of all of them except the 11th when She had a hissy fit and made the driver wait for us rather than trying to hide in the hedge again. They were both laughing so I suppose it was only pretend cross. No Agility as it was too wet and far too windy so all the jumps and equipment blow over, so a boring day though we did "twists" in the hall.

I wasn't sick in the car going to Cissbury Ring where we met Jane, Katy and Rouli, and I was let off the lead and we all ran and ran; lots and lots of people and dogs, but no problems. After about 45 minutes, I came back to have my lead put on, but She took it off again a bit later and I had another run around. Home without being sick but feeling rotten and then we had a drink and breakfast (at 11.30) and the Lawn Man came so I barked a bit, but couldn't see him as She had closed the curtains so I wasn't too stressed, then They went out for lunch. Had ribs and ball games in the garden when They got home. There was the Dog Club Christmas party tonight, which was a bit of an ordeal; very noisy and excitable, that little dog-of-a-pair never stops yapping and I could tell She was getting stressed and cross particularly as the other dogs then joined in. I was very scared by the fancy dresses as I didn't recognise the dogs and one came very near me with a big hat on, and it wasn't until the prizes had been awarded and the photos taken that I came out from behind the stage, and realised that she was my friend Star. We played Musical Newspapers (like chairs but easier for us dogs to sit on) but there was a lot of hanging around and I kept getting bored. Juliette and Tim were there and said what a different dog I was from the one they'd seen on Tuesday as when I got settled, I was really nice and lots of people cuddled me. Then They all got out the trestle tables which was very noisy and I didn't like the bumping and banging about, and brought out Their food and I got hitched to a radiator while She sat down to eat. I had never been tied up away from Her before and didn't really like it, but when I started to bark, She was very firm and said NO as if She meant it, so I thought I'd better shut up, but after a while when I had settled down, She came and got me to sit beside her chair for their meal. It seemed very late when we came home, but I won a bone as I was in the winning team for the potato-and-spoon race. I think we cheated!

What a disappointing walk in Sullington Warren today; lots of dogs about and I was off-lead, but no one wanted to play. A brown one did for a bit but then got tired and wandered off. Although I was off-lead, I did keep coming back for reassurance. I still don't like having to come into the Warren through the gate and make quite a fuss so She has to get hold of my harness and more-or-less drag me past the "danger", then everything's all right. We met lots of runners, but that was when I was still on the lead and anyway, they were too far away to get scary. I was back on the lead to cross the main road into Sandgate Park but off again to chase squirrels along the river bank and to chase the runner I chased last week. She's very nice and stops to stroke me so we're friends really, and she and She had a hug; then I was back on the lead to come home. We played box-and-cox with the postman's van in Bracken Lane; I even barked at the van when it was parked and the postman was all the way up the drive; silly me! When we got home They went very silly too; moving furniture, hoovering everywhere and bringing in a tree ~ I don't know what's going on. The tree stands in a bowl of water on the sitting room floor and I got very ticked off when I tried to drink the water; it was much more flavoursome than my usual bowl, but I think She was afraid the tree-holding mechanism might bite my nose off!

This is Sunday and I am punch drunk, counter-sunk and very, very wet, and have had the most extraordinary morning. We set off for the walk towards Sandgate Park in the wind and the rain (again) and finally reached Water Lane. We walked on the correct side of this busy road but when we got to the end, where it crosses the A283, the traffic was pouring out of Storrington and we had to wait, and wait, and wait. Eventually, we managed to cross into the lane that leads to the church, and a Huge Land Rover pulled up and asked us whether we wanted a lift to the top of the lane, so we got out of the weather and had a ride. I wasn't sick, but left muddy footprints all over the beautiful cream leather seat, and we both jumped out and went into church, again. We were filthy so sat at the back and I was so good, and the very well-dressed man beside Her said he liked dogs and didn't mind my hairs, which get everywhere, or my muddy face so I went for a bit of fussing and then lay down. There was a baptism and a few bored children in the church, so they all came and patted me, and I didn't mind, even when a little boy poked his finger through my muzzle and up my nose, She explained that I

143

didn't like that so he stroked/pulled my ears instead! I think his daddy was pleased that I was a distraction. The nice woman with the Landy offered us a lift home, so she brought us (more muddy feet) to the gate into Sandgate Park where I finally got off the lead and ran about. I didn't mind the two buggies we met, and ran with the other dogs, then, when we had crossed the bridge to come home, She called and I came back to have my lead put on. She thinks I'm wonderful, and I had lots of cheese when we got home, and then They opened the Quavers to go with the gin so we each had one of those too.

I don't know what's going on because She left really, really early today as she was going to Horsham so we didn't get breakfast or a walk, and then when She came back from there, and had done her Parking thing at the doctors' surgery, She began delivering cards through lots of letter boxes, so our walk was all on lead, up and down driveways. When the last card had gone, I sat down and demanded to go home, so as it was drizzly, we did, and had a quiet time back at home; because breakfast was about lunch time, we had our bones when it was nearly dark. What a muddly day!

Monday, 18 November 2019. I had my special collar on again. I also got very side-tracked by squirrels so lost Her and Candy so had to wait by the wood's entrance until they came back from wherever they had been as I didn't know where they were. A bit chastened.

After yesterday, I stayed close by during our walk in the woods but wouldn't be put on the lead at George's Lane to walk down the lane home, so ran by myself. The only problem was there was a garden to escape into (with chickens, but they were safely shut away) and traffic, but I still wouldn't come back. I got home after trying it on with the cross man from one of the houses; I'd never seen him before so I don't know why I didn't like him. I couldn't bite him as I had my muzzle on, but I'd have liked to try. They went out for lunch so we had a quiet day. I tried the "cross paws" trick, but only got as far as sitting up properly. Perhaps my legs aren't long enough; Candy's are much, much longer so she can do it easily. But won't.

As She went to yoga, it was Daddy's turn to walk us today and I played him up, first I did the sitting down trick, then the running away trick, so he was a bit fed up when we got home because I'd also chased a runner (who had had the sense to stop) and then a car. She gardened and I barked, but then I had to go to Her when She called, so stopped barking.

As it's Thursday, Richard came and although I barked, it wasn't as much as before. Then Kate came which was nice and I was quiet until the postman went up the lane, in a different size and colour van but I still knew it was him, and then the log man came after lunch and Daddy went to talk to him and I just barked at them. They left the side gate open to make life easier with moving the logs from the front where they had been delivered to the back where the log store is, and it wasn't supposed to be a problem because I was shut indoors. But when She went out into the garden to help him with the moving, I rushed out between her legs and was away into the front. I came back though to find a man that I didn't recognise, with a woolly hat and a wheelbarrow in the gateway, so I rushed past and tried to bite his leg from behind, as I do. I would have done if I hadn't realised that it was Daddy under the hat but I still got hold of his trousers, though not his leg, or I wouldn't be writing this now. Rather quiet all evening.

We walked in Sandgate Park today and, in spite of my new fancy recall collar, I wouldn't come back. We had a lovely walk at first; Candy and I were out in front together with Her behind, but then, coming back over the bridge I saw a man with a spaniel, and raced after him to bite his leg. I don't know why I did that. He had wellies on and I had a muzzle, but he was cross though he didn't say anything. Went on the lead to come home then. Dog school cancelled so played "'Find 'it" and ball games down the hall in the evening.

I'm still scared and having problems getting into Sullington Warren through the gate, but whatever it was that was there before seems to have gone, so it's getting a bit better. I played with the golden retriever youngster I played with last week; we remembered each other. It was a good game of chase, and even though he wouldn't go to his Mum when she called, I went to Her when She called me, which pleased us both. I had done three or four Recalls on lead first, and then a few more off, so that was good. I nearly didn't come back to have my lead put on to cross Water Lane, but then She changed direction so I did come, in case I lost her, but was off again in Sandgate Park, except at the end I ran away and nothing would make me go back to Her to have my lead on so I had a lot of fun in other people's gardens on my own way home.

It's Sunday so Daddy should have taken me out today, but he won't take me out any more, as he says I'm too unreliable and unpredictable. Two very long words I don't know the meaning of. Instead I went with Her to Sandgate Park and this is the tale of three joggers: the first one was a man She saw in the distance, She called me but I wouldn't come and just raced off to the man, but instead of him being afraid he gave me a cuddle and a fuss. When She caught up, She frightened him even more than I did by giving him a big hug and saying he was the most sensible runner She'd ever met because he wasn't scared of me; he was surprised! The second one came out of the park behind the housing estate; she was all in bright hideous yellow so I barked at her even though she gave me a wide berth, and the third one was someone who wanted to talk but kept jumping up and down so I got very anxious, and she wouldn't stop jumping so we came home. She also had on a hideous bright orange jacket ~ I think half the problem is I don't like those colours. By this time, I was scared of all the cars too, so barked and lunged at them all. Back in my cage for 12.45 when David and Anneli came for lunch and after a loud, but short, barking session, I was quiet as a mouse and everyone moved around and I didn't bother about them at all. They went home about 5.30 and I was let out of my cage and we had bones in the dark in the garden. Everyone said I was wonderful and so much better than before. Until bed time when I barked for three hours, starting at 2 am; after a while She came in to see why, but every time She went back to bed, I started again so She stayed for about three quarters of an hour and then went back to bed. So, I started again, again, and at 5 am, Daddy came in and persuaded Candy and me to come out of the conservatory so we wouldn't be upset by whatever it was that was upsetting me, and then I was quiet. Nice walk in the woods but all on lead as I was a bit twitchy. Bones in the rain.

We had such a good walk in Sandgate Park where I ran off-lead and came back when She stopped to talk to a woman with a chocolate lab. I had my lead put on and didn't mind the cars, or even the horses we met on the way home as long as we could get a long way into the driveways to escape. Still a bit scared of the narrow twitten, not made any better by a man coming up behind us and scaring us all as he tried to get past, so I pulled hard on the lead, but he got away. They went out for lunch and as it was still raining when they got back, it was a very quiet day.

Wednesday, 27th. The milkman came again during the night, this time delivering to Cyril at 3.30, so I barked and barked and woke everyone up. I then kept barking for about 35 minutes until She shouted at me to stop, so I did, eventually. As She was determined to go to yoga, Daddy had to walk me which neither of us liked; he was in such a mood and had shouted at Her during breakfast so I stayed in my cage for as long as I could. For the walk, I got as far as the end of the drive before I sat down, and then wouldn't budge again at the end of the lane before the twitten, so he brought me back and took Candy out instead. I stayed at home on my own when She'd gone out. He doesn't seem to like me at all anymore and it's getting very difficult.

We had a lovely walk in Sandgate Park today even though it was so wet. I still wouldn't come back to have my lead put on though. I put up a pheasant in someone's garden so was off along the gardens to see what else I could find. I got caught in the end, but She was very glad no one could see us being so naughty. I was good at Agility/Flyball but there is a problem because if I'm off-lead, I will run away with the ball and not bring it back, and if I'm on lead, I won't bother even to pick the ball up as I can't run with it. A high-visibility jogger ran along the path on the other side of the next field, so miles away, and I got really upset and growled and barked, and Jay

148

the teacher said she'd never seen me like that, particularly as the person was so far away; not a lot wrong with my eyesight then.

We met Rebecca and Alfie this morning so walked together, but I wouldn't come back at the end, and chased off along Badgers Holt all through the gardens. I was caught in the end by the nice old man who has biscuits. We went to School in the evening which was very hard as there were lots of noisy and badly behaved dogs there, including two powder puffs with no legs that yapped for the whole hour. The woman who owned them couldn't manage one, let alone two; I could feel Her getting crosser and crosser. Then there was a sort-of collie, filthy dirty, who growled and grumbled and made me very scared, but by the end I was doing weaving in and out of the dogs including that one, and it all settled down. I got a prize for being good, though She said I didn't deserve it, and neither of us could remember what I had done to get it. At the end of class, She threw the tuggy for me, and I chased after it, shook it to death and then brought it back and She and I played tuggy, a first as I've not done that before. She has taken to wearing a bright high viz jacket which she "borrowed, with permission" from the doctors' surgery who are having building work done so there was one spare, to see if I'm bothered by it at home, but I'm not, not at all. It's the tension emitted by the runners that unnerves me, because I don't mind children running about in fun.

As it was a Saturday, we had no breakfast as Daddy took us to Sullington Warren in his car, and I had a lovely run there in spite of a very cross man shouting at Her to keep me under control (and I hadn't done anything except bark) but fortunately Doreen was there to be a witness, as he was very threatening, and one of the men we had been talking to before came over and asked Her if she was all right. They didn't like his body language either. So, for safety, I went on the extending lead for the rest of the way home where we met a jogger round the corner where Hampers and Bracken Lanes meet, I barked and she jumped, but we ended up friends and she stroked me and said what lovely soft fur I had. When we got home, Heather came round for her newspaper and a cup of coffee whilst I stayed in my cage. In the afternoon, I had a bone whilst She raked the leaves up.

****

3 November

Hello Ann,

I'm sorry it sounds so tough for you still and your vet was not that helpful but I guess they are so busy that you can only resort to behaviourists for strategies.

I have had two dogs that needed to be muzzled and I can only say that my rule is that it goes on the minute they step out of the house and comes off when they come in. There can be no deviations because it just confuses them and in my case my dog has already nipped the postman and if he caught another postie or delivery man, the police would just come and take him away.

And she should not be squabbling with her housemate! I hope they make up and get over it.

Hopefully, the next chapter will be more positive.

V

****

29 November

Dear Friend

We don't get breakfast when Daddy takes us to Sandgate Park in the car as Dizzy is car sick, so we had a lovely breakfast about lunch time when we got back from our walk. Thank you for the delicious meal we had today …. please will you go out for lunch again soon so we can have more meals wrapped in silver paper?

With love

Candy and Dizzy

Reply:

30 November

Dear Candy & Dizzy

You are most welcome!

I was going to write and thank your Mummy and Daddy properly for a lovely lunch. It was such a treat to be taken out and it was very kind.

Much love to you both and Mummy and Daddy

We had a lovely lunch; I just could not finish all of mine but I am glad you enjoyed what I had left. It was lovely to see

them both and I hope we can all go out again soon both
enjoyed it – liver is very good for you

Your friend Xxxx

Chapter Eleven

December

The Crisis

Sunday, 1 December 2019. I went to church, a different one; Daddy took us a bit of the way so I wouldn't be too muddy when we arrived, and we walked the rest along pathways. I wasn't sure about the sound of the bells, but they were quieter inside, so we went in even though it was early and I got used to the hum of the organ playing quietly and the sound of all the people coming in. I got lots of pats and fusses and everyone thought I was lovely, but it was the church itself that was so calming and serene that I couldn't be scared because there was no threat from anywhere. She sat down for the whole morning, even though the other people got up to sing and move about, and there were a lot of Christingle candles and sweets, but I wasn't allowed them; however, I did have my own treats. I didn't like going into the wooden cage with the bench that She sat on, but for a lot of the time we had it to ourselves, then a churchwarden came and sat at the end. During the morning, I got bored and wanted to go home so I went towards the man who was in the way and bumped his leg very gently with my nose, but he wouldn't move so I went back to where I had been and lay down. We splashed our way home through the mud at the end after a lot more fussing, and Her putting her boots back on, and came home in time for their lunch and our breakfast, and then bones afterwards.

Monday; a strange man with a hat on was walking round the outside of the conservatory so I barked and growled and went crazy without realising it was Daddy. I don't like his hat. I don't like people so close to the window.

I think there must have been some email correspondence because after a short walk with Her, Mark-of-the-sprats came round and they had a long talk, about me, so I sat up in my cage and looked cute. They were supposed to be talking about Recall, but Mark simply said the problem needed managing. What problem? Daddy brought Candy back from their walk, but took his hat off before he came in, and then he talked to Mark as well.

As She went to yoga, I went to Barking Success, but I went on my own as Candy was out with Daddy, and I didn't like it without her, so when I got home again, I sat on Daddy's feet and wouldn't move all afternoon so he wouldn't lose me while She was gardening, and all evening as well. Did lots of Sendaways in the hall, and will now bring my ball back so She can throw it again. Played ball in the garden which was still frosty.

Walk in Sandgate Park on the flexi and I did three Recalls there and one on the way home. I also didn't bark at any of the cars, but that was because we managed to get out of the way up people's driveways in time. Agility in the afternoon, where I did well on lead but ran away and wouldn't come back off-lead. So back on the lead and very boring!!!

It is Saturday again so we drove to Sullington Warren where I had a crisis at the gate, again; months ago, there was a man and two dogs in the gateway and I got scared, so now won't go through the gate, or along the path. We met two different collies at the gate, and another dog and I still wouldn't budge until She lifted me up by the harness and physically moved me on. Then we were all right until we got to the next gateway where I had met the cross runner last week so I got stuck again. She had to move me by my harness again, but then it was all right as I met the dog I had chased before in the wide green space, and we chased again. And again. It was such fun and then I came back and had my lead put back on as everyone went in different directions. The first runners we met in Badger's Close were so far away at first that She had time to rein me in and we waited on the verge until they had passed, which was lovely, but a bit further on we met two silly women who wouldn't give me space and continued running in spite of the fact that She asked them to walk past as I had managed to extend the Flexi to its maximum as her hands hurt so much she couldn't control the run of the lead. One of the women who was scared stiff stopped still, but the other continued jumping up and down so I chased her off. If only they would just stand still until we are past. Lots of nasty words from her. Got back home exhausted, but no further incidents; I ignored the flock of Jacobs even though one of them was head-butting the feed bucket. Silly sheep.

Something different today; I went to Barking Success paddock on my own for a training session with Her but it was very strange and I didn't like it; I didn't have Candy as support and I was very scared of the fence-corner and refused to go there, even pulling myself out of my collar and lead when She tried to make me. I did a lot of dribbling and wouldn't go far enough away for any Recall training to be any use. Once again, I slept on Daddy's feet for the rest of the day.

We met Jenny (who also has rescue dogs) in the woods, and while She was talking to her, I slipped my harness and was off, chasing squirrels, of which there were plenty, and two big cows who ran away. The cows are there to eat the prickly brambles and spiky bracken and only come for a few weeks each year; She says it would have been a good thing if they had kicked me to teach me who to respect, which I think is rather unkind, but cows released in public places have to be good with people and dogs so, of course, they wouldn't kick me. Eventually, I came back and was back on the lead and we came home, but after lunch we went to Kate's and I did Recalls in her garden; I was very good at it and even came when Kate called, which surprised everyone. Then They had tea and began to prepare to come home; this included breaking up clumps of yellow daisies as Kate had told Her she was welcome to some; I was all right until they began to chop the clumps with a spade which I didn't like as I got frightened. So I ran at Kate, and head butted her with my muzzle, which was very naughty and made Her cross but everything calmed down in the end and we came home. I slept all evening.

As the cows are still in the woods I was on lead, though She let me off when we'd left them far behind. But I know these woods and wouldn't come back so when we got home, She said we weren't going in there again and would have to walk somewhere else, where I didn't run away. She spent the whole day cooking (lovely smells) and totally ignored me except when She dropped some cheese on the floor.

We went to Barking Success this morning as Daddy still won't take me out; her car smelled of cheese and garlic as She was taking food to the yoga class lunch party. We didn't want to go into BS at first and when we went into the open space I ran to the wire to watch her drive away, and barked and barked in despair but it was all right as Daddy came and collected us and brought us home a bit later. He was in the garden putting up some lights so we had to stay inside as it wasn't safe to have us and ladders, and then She came home and it started to rain, again, so we all had a quiet afternoon and evening.

Thursday, 19 December. A day I won't forget. I was being very particular as to where I wanted Her to take me today; I wasn't going to go down the very wet twitten as I wanted to go down the road so I could see the ducks on one side of the road and make them quack, and the pheasants on the other to make them fly. As She had me on a lead this was all very frustrating, so I sat down and wouldn't go anywhere at all. Then we met the nice people with the black lab (yes, another one) and I went over to see them and forgot to sulk, so we came home via the Jacobs sheep and the road. When we got back, She went into a frenzy of cleaning, and I kept being chased about to avoid the Henry-the-Hoover, so went to sit in the safety of my cage. At about 11, Heather came round to sort out Her computer problems and she said I could come out of my cage as I was so calm, so She let me out and Heather and I had a lot of fussing and stroking. Eventually, they went into the office but it's a narrow space between the kitchen and office doors, so when Daddy came out of the kitchen too, with Candy, I just couldn't cope in the congested apace and had The Panic Attack Red Mist again and went for Heather; both legs. One was a bad bite, the other not so bad, and She had to find the TCP and dressings to sort her out. There was blood on the office floor. After Heather had gone home, She made a couple of phone calls, and was very upset. They were out at a party this evening so we had a quiet time in.

The next day, we walked in Sandgate Park and I did three Recalls on lead, complete with handbrake turns, but wouldn't come back when off-lead. However, She did manage to catch me in the end, but I didn't mind as I was very muddy and wet. When we got home, we had games with the drying-off towel and then She cleaned the sitting room and I sat in my cage getting warm and dry as the Aga is on full, so the kitchen is lovely and warm. She keeps the hall door closed to stop Candy shaking all over the hall paintwork, so neither of us can get out and it's lovely and cosy. The men came to cut down the last of the not-wanted trees; I barked a bit but She had closed the conservatory blinds so I couldn't see them and I got bored so began to ignore them, and then they went home leaving a big pile of logs. We all had a very late lunch and then She dashed off again in the car, but was home in time for a cup of tea. I am beginning to think that I can be a proper dog as I try to be really good, except for The Biting Problem.

20 December, written to the behaviourist concerning the biting. His reply:

Many thanks for your email. You really need to ensure that she is not set up to fail, so be very careful about the off lead times… She does seem to be improving all the time though.

I wouldn't allow anyone to stroke her in enclosed places as this may cause her more stress… You really need to write all these logs down and maybe get them published…

Regards,

Mark

Epilogue

Friday afternoon. Andy the vet rang to say that he could fit us in at 5.30 pm when he got back from surgery in Steyning, so I put Dizzy in the car on a lead, and had the muzzle in my hand. We got in through the vet's door and she went to sit on the scales just like she always does (she's gained a bit more weight) and everyone else in the waiting room (even the couple with a cat) thought she was so cute and pretty. It broke my heart. When Andy called us in, his opening remark was along the lines of "you don't need to feel guilty; I've been expecting you for a few months now". While we were discussing things, the senior partner of the practice came in to collect some dressings or drugs or something, and he and Andy agreed with me that there was no other option; Andy said that whilst he was convinced in his decision, it was nice to have his view backed up by another vet, particularly as one of the reception staff had suggested asking the behaviourist and/or rescue kennels for advice, which wasn't really helping things. Andy gave her lots of treats as he injected a type of pre-med into her scruff and she gradually got sleepy and relaxed so that he could go and get the electric clippers and the real injection, but when he came back with everything, at the whizzing sound of the clippers she was wide awake again and very panicky, so he switched off the noise and just clipped the fur of her front leg with a pair of scissors, which were silent and therefore all right. It just showed how tense she really was, even when we thought she was calm and relaxed she was never really "switched off". During the sitting-on-the-floor period, I said to Andy that knowing hearing was the last sense to go, I must not cry as long as she could hear me. Eventually, he looked up and said, "You can cry now; she's gone." I have hardly stopped crying since.

It wasn't supposed to end like this, we knew it was going to be hard work and a long haul, but she was getting so much better. Whilst I could manage most situations, I couldn't manage other people. Every time she nipped or bit someone, I could rationalise why, and make excuses, as you already know. It is so easy to be wise after the event, but the events often happen so quickly that there is no time to take evading action. The episode in the hall was simply that she could cope with two humans and herself in the narrow space of only 45 inches wide, but when Tony came as well with Candy in tow, it was just too much for her. I realise that now; but didn't think to ask him to stay with her in the conservatory. How much longer should I have allowed this to go on? I thought it was better to take action now with a vet I knew and we both trusted than to wait for someone to complain to the police again, and have the matter taken out of my hands, and possibly out of my vet's hands too.

I can't help feeling that I have failed her, even though I know she had ten months here that were happy and free of anxiety most of the time; whether her Red Mist was a congenital thing or a result of dreadful experiences in the four years before we met, I don't know. What I do know is that the unpredictability of it was what worried me most, and, not knowing what caused it, it was hard to correct, prevent or side-track. One person we met at Dog School, who had seen her protective and tense at home, said she couldn't believe it was the same dog, perhaps she should have been placed with a hermit on a hill, but there aren't a lot of them about round here these days.

This whole experience has also raised a question about the ethicacy of importing dogs from Eastern Europe, or anywhere else for that matter. It has been brought to my notice, though without any concrete evidence, that these dogs are the product of puppy farms in these countries who see it as a good way to make money out of the "caring English" and presumably caring others too. This idea has been suggested and accepted by quite a lot of people who have known and had dealings with these rescue dogs; they can't prove it either but the evidence seems to be there. I have always had theoretical problems with imported rescue dogs believing that we have quite a lot of dogs in this country that need homes, and that the money spent on getting these dogs passports, spayed or castrated, transported, inoculated and rehomed could be better spent here. Some of them are so damaged that I don't believe life here can be much fun for them even when they have been "rescued". I thought I had experience (I had, but not enough) and I worry what happens to those dogs who just can't adjust and are returned again and again to the rescue kennels. I was prepared for Dizzy to have to have a muzzle on every time we went out, but drew the line on her having to have one on when she was at home too because we never knew when someone was going to arrive unexpectedly. Mark the behaviourist and Rhia said that we couldn't cure her, we'd just have to manage the situation, I will never forgive myself for failing to manage.

And as every day passes, this guilt gets worse as the drama subsides and the reality of what I have done persists. I still expect to see her sitting at the side of my chair as I type, and have to check that she's not too close so I don't run over her feet when I push my chair back from the desk. We've washed the blankets and put her bowl away, but her presence is here all the time as she was such a dear and lovely character. I don't yet know how I am going to tell all the wonderful people who have helped me with her transformation towards an English village dog who plays ball and tuggy, runs a Flyball course and curls into such a very small ball by the sofa; they will be as distressed as we are.

She is buried in the garden, by the oak tree with the squirrels in, and Candy goes and visits her sometimes.

A Few Thoughts

I sent the above Epilogue to a friend (who had had one of my puppies many years ago) as my explanation of what had happened and why, and why I would only be meeting her with one dog, not two, and she asked me if she could forward my email to a friend of hers who had gone through a similar traumatic decision, and also felt guilty that she hadn't managed to "solve" all her dog's problems. It appears that I'm not the only one who ends up with dogs from "abroad" who have insurmountable difficulties, and I am concerned that having got "Lucy's Law" onto the Statute Book, those who used to profit from puppy farming in this country will now turn to "importing rescue dogs" to make their money. A case of "unintended consequences".

During Dizzy's time with us, a number of questions have arisen with regard to the law, so, having been told different things by different people, I wrote to The Kennel Club:

"I had a Romanian street dog rescue who was very defensive/aggressive; because she had nipped many of the volunteers at the rescue kennels, I was asked to keep her muzzled for a year. It was only when people kept asking me why she had a muzzle on that I was informed of the "regulations" about leads and lead lengths for a muzzled dog. I was told that if a dog had a muzzle on, she also had to be on a lead at all times when out and the length of that lead was specified. I was working on her Recall ~ she was good when she knew she had no alternative i.e. in the garden, on a lead, on a training lead, but less reliable when it was a toss-up between me and a squirrel ~ the squirrel usually won! But I need her off-lead in order to confirm that she will come when called. I can't find any reference online for this guidance, and would be grateful for your advice."

Their reply:

"If you have in effect voluntarily decided to muzzle your dog, (or in this instance on the advice of staff at the rescue kennels), then there is no linked requirement regarding a lead.

Some dogs which come to the attention of the police, can be subject to court orders which require both a lead and a muzzle to be used in public. Most commonly these requirements are placed on owners of pit bull terriers. In those cases the dogs have been assessed by the courts to be safe to keep as pets, but are required to muzzled and kept on a lead as a precautionary measure. There are also powers for council officers to place similar restrictions on dogs which come to their attention.

In either case I would've advised discussing the matter with the respective enforcement agency. However, in your case as it appears to be a voluntary muzzling measure then I would suggest there is no requirement to use a lead.

I'm slightly concerned as to the advice you've received to keep your dog muzzled for a year, as this seems to be a rather arbitrary figure. I would encourage you to speak to a dog trainer or behaviourist and ask them to assess your dog to check whether the muzzle remains appropriate or whether there are other steps you can take to socialise your dog."

****

I have found it impossible to get a straight answer from anyone about the subject of having "dangerous" dogs put to sleep. As far as I can see, it is up to the local authority or the local police to make arrangements, so, as Dizzy already had a police record from way back, I was afraid that she would be taken away and put to sleep by someone in the police or local authority, who neither of us would know. She would have been terrified, and bitten and fought, so would have had to have a muzzle which would make her worse. That was why I decided to take matters into my, and my vet's, hands; she knew us and was happy and unmuzzled with us, and had as good an end as I could create.

****

There is something else which has come to light since Dizzy went, and that's the reaction of Candy. Dizzy exuded often unseen tension and anxiety and only after she had gone did, I realise that Candy had reacted to this tension; after a month or so, her tail was back and wagging as she walked, she ventured further into the fields, and she relaxed, really relaxed. In all the turmoil of Dizzy's life, I had overlooked how much Candy had taken on board. That was my mistake. It took a neighbour to comment, after about nine months, that "this" was the first time Candy had gone to her for a stroke and a fuss; in the past, she had allowed her to come to her, but wouldn't make the first move. This time, though, Candy approached the neighbour, and to my shame, I hadn't really noticed this change of behaviour. I have a friend whose friend's second child was disabled, the family were so worried about the disabled child that the older one had to fend for herself and carried the scars of what she felt was rejection well into middle life. I think in a way I fell into the same trap. Many people now say how young and enthusiastic Candy is, in spite of her 12+ years, and looks much younger than she used to do.

We never see the whole picture when we make a decision, whether to move house, get married or buy a dog, and as I found out, there was a lot more to getting this rescue dog than I had imagined, Candy having been so easy by comparison. Don't let me put you off, just remember that it's a full-on experience, and the more you put into it the better the experience is.